A Life of Islam

A LIFE
IS^{OF}LAM

Yamin Cheng

TOP

The Other Press
Kuala Lumpur

Published by
The Other Press Sdn. Bhd.
607 Mutiara Majestic
Jalan Othman
46000 Petaling Jaya
Selangor, Malaysia
www.ibtbooks.com

The Other Press is affiliated with Islamic Book Trust.

Perpustakaan Negara Malaysia   Cataloguing-in-Publication Data

Cheng, Yamin
    A Life Of Islam / Yamin Cheng.
    ISBN 978-967-0957-27-2
    1. Religious life--Islam.
    2. Islam--Customs and practices.
    3. Muslims--Conduct of life.
    I. Title.
    297.57

Printed by
Vinlin Press Sdn. Bhd.
No. 2, Jalan Meranti Permai 1
Meranti Permai Industrial Park
Batu 15, Jalan Puchong
47100 Puchong, Selangor D.E.

Contents

Preface vii

Surah (Chapters) in the Qur'an... ix

The Sacred and Human Life... 1

A Life of God 7

A Life with a Centre... 11

A Life of Purpose... 15

Life as *Khalifah* 21

A Life of Worship.. 26

A Life of Prayer... 30

A Life of Purity.. 36

A Life of Virtue.. 41

A Life of Sincerity... 44

A Life of Culture.. 53

A Life of Togetherness.. 57

Life with Nature 62

A Life of Thought... 67

A Life of Inquiry... 71

A Life of Learning 76

A Life of Work.. 82

A Life of Guidance 91

A Life of Solitude... 100

Life Goes On 107

A Life of Both Worlds.. 110

A Life of Religion 115

A Life of Islam 121

A Chinese Life of Islam 128

A Life Worth Asking About 138

Index 141

Preface

A life of Islam is a life that blossoms from God, who is addressed as *Allah*, from where all things wise and wonderful, bright and beautiful, as well as blessed and delightful come into this colourful world.

From *Allah*, a Muslim derives his sense of identity as a human being with regard to his beliefs, actions, thoughts and cultural expressions.

This book attempts to show what a life of Islam is like and in what ways God's presence in our life makes us into the kind of human being we humans desire.

The contents of this book are drawn from a host of writings that the author has penned, whether they were published or yet to be published, and these were put together to present a general picture of the life of Islam.

On a personal level, this book serves as a reference point for the author's other writings, whether those that have been written or the ones to be written, so that the author will have a clear idea with regard to how his thoughts and ideas are related to one another as well as sewn into each other and how, together, they can present the author's view on Islam in a broader perspective.

Yamin Cheng

Surah (Chapters) in the Qur'an

1. Al-Fatihah (the Opening)
2. Al-Baqarah (the Cow)
3. Aali Imran (the Family of Imran)
4. An-Nisa' (the Women)
5. Al-Ma'idah (the Table)
6. Al-An'am (the Cattle)
7. Al-A'raf (the Heights)
8. Al-Anfal (the Spoils of War)
9. At-Taubah (the Repentance)
10. Yunus (Yunus)
11. Hud (Hud)
12. Yusuf (Yusuf)
13. Ar-Ra'd (the Thunder)
14. Ibrahim (Ibrahim)
15. Al-Hijr (the Rocky Tract)
16. An-Nahl (the Bees)
17. Al-Isra' (the Night Journey)
18. Al-Kahf (the Cave)
19. Maryam (Maryam)
20. Ta-Ha (Ta-Ha)
21. Al-Anbiya' (the Prophets)
22. Al-Haj (the Pilgrimage)
23. Al-Mu'minun (the Believers)
24. An-Nur (the Light)
25. Al-Furqan (the Criterion)
26. Ash-Shu'ara' (the Poets)
27. An-Naml (the Ants)

28. Al-Qasas (the Stories)
29. Al-Ankabut (the Spider)
30. Ar-Rum (the Romans)
31. Luqman (Luqman)
32. As-Sajdah (the Prostration)
33. Al-Ahzab (the Combined Forces)
34. Saba' (the Sabeans)
35. Al-Fatir (the Originator)
36. Ya-Sin (Ya-Sin)
37. As-Saffah (Those Ranges in Ranks)
38. Sad (Sad)
39. Az-Zumar (the Groups)
40. Ghafir (the Forgiver)
41. Fusilat (Distinguished)
42. Ash-Shura (the Consultation)
43. Az-Zukhruf (the Gold)
44. Ad-Dukhan (the Smoke)
45. Al-Jathiyah (the Kneeling)
46. Al-Ahqaf (the Valley)
47. Muhammad (Muhammad)
48. Al-Fath (the Victory)
49. Al-Hujurat (the Dwellings)
50. Qaf (Qaf)
51. Adz-Dzariyat (the Scatterers)
52. At-Tur (the Mount)
53. An-Najm (the Star)
54. Al-Qamar (the Moon)
55. Ar-Rahman (the Most Gracious)
56. Al-Waqi'ah (the Event)
57. Al-Hadid (the Iron)
58. Al-Mujadilah (the Reasoning)
59. Al-Hashr (the Gathering)
60. Al-Mumtahanah (the Tested)
61. As-Saf (the Row)
62. Al-Jum'ah (Friday)
63. Al-Munafiqun (the Hypocrites)
64. At-Taghabun (the Loss & Gain)
65. At-Talaq (the Divorce)
66. At-Tahrim (the Prohibition)
67. Al-Mulk (the Kingdom)
68. Al-Qalam (the Pen)
69. Al-Haqqah (the Inevitable)
70. Al-Ma'arij (the Elevated Passages)
71. Nuh (Nuh)
72. Al-Jinn (the Jinn)

73. Al-Muzammil (the Wrapped)
74. Al-Mudaththir (the Cloaked)
75. Al-Qiyamah (the Resurrection)
76. Al-Insan (the Human)
77. Al-Mursalat (Those Sent Forth)
78. An-Naba' (the Great News)
79. An-Nazi'at (Those Who Pull Out)
80. 'Abasa (He Frowned)
81. At-Takwir (the Overthrowing)
82. Al-Infitar (the Cleaving)
83. Al-Mutaffifin (Those Who Deal in Fraud)
84. Al-Inshiqaq (the Splitting Asunder)
85. Al-Buruj (the Stars)
86. At-Tariq (the Nightcomer)
87. Al-A'la (the Most High)
88. Al-Ghashiyah (the Overwhelming)
89. Al-Fajr (the Dawn)
90. Al-Balad (the City)
91. Ash-Shams (the Sun)
92. Al-Layl (the Night)
93. Adh-Dhuha (the Forenoon)
94. Al-Inshirah (the Opening Forth)
95. At-Tin (the Fig)
96. Al-'Alaq (the Clot)
97. Al-Qadar (the Night of Decree)
98. Al-Bayinah (the Proof)
99. Az-Zalzalah (the Earthquake)
100. Al-'Adiyah (the Runners)
101. Al-Qari'ah (the Striking Hour)
102. At-Takathur (the Piling Up)
103. Al-'Asr (the Time)
104. Al-Humazah (the Slanderer)
105. Al-Fil (the Elephant)
106. Quraish (Quraish)
107. Al-Ma'un (the Assistance)
108. Al-Kauthar (the River of Abundance)
109. Al-Kafirun (the

Disbelievers)   112. Al-Ikhlas (the Sincerity)
110. An-Nasr (the Help)   113. Al-Falaq (the Daybreak)
111. Al-Masad (the Palm   114. An-Nas (Mankind)
    Fiber)

Note:

1. There is no official translation of the meaning of the Qur'an. There are several translations of the meaning of the Qur'an into English but the one that is quite widely used is that by Abdullah Yusuf Ali.

2. As far as this book is concerned, the author tries to provide his own translation but the translation by Abdullah Yusuf Ali is consulted whenever the author wishes to use another translation.

3. Citation of the Qur'an is represented as Q2:112 meaning Quran, surah or chapter 2, verse or ayah 112, and so on and so forth.

1

The Sacred and Human Life

Prophet Muhammad, Islam's messenger of God said, 'Every child is born in his *fitrah* (our inborn nature, such as, for instance, an adopted child's longing to know his real parents even though he has been separated from them since birth). By way of his parents, he secures his identity, whether a Jew, a Christian, or a Magian.' And, for that matter, a Buddhist, a Hindu, a Shinto, a Confucian, or a Taoist, to name some others.

We come into this world through our parents and obviously whatever path of life our parents take, we too follow that path, until such time when we are mature enough to make decisions of our own regarding our life's path. Notwithstanding, any path of life that is a good path is one that brings out our *fitrah*—those jolly-good elements of our soul, conscience, and inner voice—into our life's activities, and make us desirable human beings. Even when one or both parents have swerved from life's ideal path, their *fitrah* would not permit them to do the same to their children, for a father who steals would not advise his children to do the same. As such, while we may embrace different ways of living, we cannot suppress, reject, or deny our *fitrah* that is our human nature. A person who is disobedient to his parents and ignorant of his religion, would somehow, be guided by his *fitrah* in his conduct of life, even if he had committed things that are unbecoming, as feeling regretful for the unpleasant things we did is surely a sign of our good-natured *fitrah*.

◆

An essential aspect of our *fitrah* is our tendency for the sacred. Human beings, since the beginning of history, have always felt that their existence is not complete nor fulfilling if they do not feel a sense of sacredness in them and the things around them. Different societies interpret sacredness differently. Some societies, such as the primitive people, see sacredness in the natural environment that they inhabit. Primitive people depend on the natural environment for food, shelter, and clothing, but they have always felt that certain forces are dwelling and moving in their natural habitat and unless appeased, these forces could disrupt their living condition. Not knowing what these forces are and where they come from, these people feel that there are boundaries in the natural environment upon which they should not intrude, otherwise, these forces would be stirred from their domain of quietude and move in the direction of their human counterparts.

Not only primitive people, but people in all times and

places, have always perceived the natural environment to be a *mysterium tremendum et fascinans*—a mysterious presence that seems to astound its human inhabitants, either with its beauty and usefulness, or with its wrath and prowess.

Nature is at once the image of a beautiful lady as well as that of an angry man. The ancient Greeks, for instance, despite their civilizational achievements, thought that the world they lived in was full of gods—male and female. Zeus was the chief god, Poseidon was the god of the seas, and Hades was the god of the underworld. Asteria was the goddess of the stars, and Artemis was the goddess of the hunt, Nature, and birth. The gods and goddesses ruled the world, but they also fought among themselves.

The Chinese, on the other hand, see their world as inhabited by dead ancestors. These ancestors, after their demise, went on to become guardians of the living. They communicate with their living ones through the proper rituals that their living ones administered for them. For the Chinese, human beings are not just ordinary beings. They can turn into sacred beings once they die.

◆

Sensing sacredness evokes in us the regard and respect for the things we see, touch, and feel. But as humans, we have the tendency to stretch our regard for these things beyond what they are, that these things carry a certain divinity we bind ourselves to, or even worship, for that matter. We see in stones and woods, fire and water—their power for our utility, and yet we also see that their power can loom over our psychology to the extent that we regard them as something to be fearful of. The Chinese think that things, incidents, and even numbers have sacred elements that carry good and bad omen. Just like some Westerners who regard '13' as an unlucky number, the Chinese see '4' as an unlucky number because the number sounds like death in Chinese, and therefore, the Chinese would avoid having the number for their car plates, for instance, in case some mishap might happen to them because of the power the number carries.

Our inability to cope and deal with the many complexities and questions surrounding our human existence was said, by some, as the reason that has turned us in the direction of an outside source for answers. A person who fears that his boat will sink in the face of a wave, for instance, has the courage to believe that his boat will not sink because there is some kind of supernatural or divine intervention coming from somewhere 'out there' to appease the wave and make his boat safe. Such is the unique character of the human species that without sacredness, life is unthinkable, and civilization unrealizable.

◆

It goes without saying that in the face of the human attachment for the sacred, things of Nature as well as human beings could assume and manifest supernatural power and loom over the fate and destiny of humans.

Such however is not the case with Islam. Things that come and go, blossom and wither, live and die, cannot be identified as the sacred and become the ground of reality. When the Prophet passed away, some of the companions could not accept this news and started to behave erratically. Abu Bakr, the Prophet's closest companion as well as the first caliph of Islam, had to calm these people down. Abu Bakr told them, 'If you worship Muhammad, know that Muhammad is dead. But if you worship God, know that God is alive.'

The Tao-Te Ching, a foundation thought of Chinese civilization, says, 'Humans model upon earth, earth models upon heaven, heaven models upon the Way, and the Way models upon what has existed since time immemorial.'

Hinduism speaks of Brahman, the reason for all existence. However, Brahman cannot be described as to what it is and yet, it is everywhere and nowhere, everything and nothing. A Hindu who looks at a tree sees not only a tree, but sees Brahman by which the existence of the tree becomes possible.

Even Plato and Aristotle, two very important Greek thinkers whose thoughts have impacted both Western and Islamic civilizations, came to the conclusion that behind everything that exists, there is a source behind their existence. Plato calls this source the Form, and everything that exists in this world is a carbon-copy of a form that is carried into their physical existence. A flower may grow, wither and die but the flower's form exists forever and although all flowers come and go, the 'flower' as an independent reality, the 'abstract' flower so to speak, continues to exist and through it, all flowers in their physical appearance come into existence.

Aristotle thinks that things move from the material to the immaterial, that whatever we see, touch, and feel will move in the direction of the abstract and ending in a supreme mind which is theos or god. The world, being a material substance, is impure but thought is pure and therefore life, for humans, is to move from bodily pleasures to pleasures of the mind which will eventually connect the human mind to the supreme mind that is the purest of purities and which is none other than god.

For Plato and Aristotle, material things are impure whereas non-material things, such as thought, are pure. Therefore, the life of a human being is to move from impurity to purity, from material concerns of life to spiritual concerns of life, from satisfaction of sensual desires to satisfaction in knowledge of first principles.

Needless to say, things of Nature, as well as human beings, cannot assume the identity of the sacred or become the ground of reality. The sacred and the ground of reality must be that which is not immersed by impurity nor coloured by profanity and ephemerality. And what would this be? For Muslims, it is God, it is *Allah*.

2

A Life of God

A life of Islam is a life centred on *tawhid*, namely, God as the centre of one's worldview, values, and activities. Muslims address God by the name *Allah* and it is through *Allah* that a Muslim derives his sense and purpose of existence, realizes his identity as a human being, and organizes his life's conduct and activities. Needless to say, for a Muslim, *Allah* is the source by which a Muslim blossoms into his human meaning, carries that meaning into his everyday living, and from which he is able to grow into a wholesome human being.

Because *Allah* is the centre through which the Muslim derives his sense of identity as well as direction in life, therefore whenever he looks at the world, he sees everything and everywhere echoing the presence of the Divine. 'And turn wherever you may, the presence of *Allah* surely stays,' says the Qur'an, Islam's book of guidance, in surah (chapter) al-Baqarah verse 115 (Q2:115). For a Muslim, the world is a wonder of many things, and no matter how it appears to an onlooker, it always speaks of God, of *Allah*. This is called *tawhid*.

For a Muslim, God is *tawhid*—one, only, and unique. God is not like any other. God does not resemble creatures, be they humans or animals, or their representations in pictures and stones. Instead, all things, living and non-living, as well as events, incidents, or even accidents, are signs pointing back to God as their source of existence, or occurrence.

Tawhid or God's oneness is the oneness of His self-image but its oneness does not stop there. Its oneness also includes His power and dominion, as well as His other attributes, such as sympathy, serenity, beauty, majesty, and many more, which are collectively put as 'the ninety-nine attributes of *Allah*.' Thus it is not sufficient to regard *Allah* as the supreme reality without also acknowledging His ownership of the vast spectrum of creation. *Allah* cannot only be adored and that is all to His identity while humans are free to take charge of their destiny with no interference from Him.

The proper way to acknowledge *Allah* is to acknowledge that He is the maker of life but He is also its caretaker. As such, *Allah* is *at once* God, Lord, and Abundance. He is *Al-Ilah* (God-ship as object of recognition of oneness, adoration, and commitment), *Al-Rabb* (Lord-ship as life-giver, caretaker, and sustainer), and *Al-Asma' wa Al-Sifat* (Abundance as, among others, majesty, splendour, grace, wisdom, mercy, love, virtue, and beauty).

Through the heart attaching, the mind reflecting, the body doing, and the person living, we bring ourselves in touch with *Allah*, about who He *is*, what He *means* to our existence, and what He *does* for us humans. For a Muslim, *Allah* is everything to him. For him, *Allah* is the centre of everything.

It is *Allah* that his existence is possible. It is *Allah* that life has a purpose. It is *Allah* who provides his sustenance. It is *Allah* who rolls out his providence. When he wakes up from sleep, he says '*Alhamdulillah*,' thanking *Allah* for the life he continues having. When he does a thing, he says '*Bismillah*' at the beginning of what he is doing, imploring the blessings of *Allah* for his quest of living. When he gets his wishes fulfilled, he says '*Syukur lillah*,' remembering that it is *Allah* who grants his longings. When he looks at the grandeurs of Nature's design, he says '*SubhanAllah*,' praising *Allah* for the beauty that mesmerizes the eyes that are watching. When he missteps his life's doings, he says '*Astaghfirullah*,' hoping that *Allah* will gloss over his misdoings.

When he wakes up and opens his eyes, he remembers *Allah* who gifted him yet another chance at life to see what good he would make out of it. When he puts on his clothes, he remembers *Allah* who gifted him the liking for beauty so that he may look handsome (or pretty) and lovely and then asks himself, 'Will I be beautiful and lovely in my character too?' When he takes his cup of coffee or tea, he remembers *Allah* who gifted water for him to make it into many kinds of drinks that are sweet and tasty but that they should make him healthy and not the opposite. When he goes to school or his workplace, he remembers *Allah* who gifted him the passion and ambition to learn and to be a useful person who can contribute to the well-being of himself and others but that being a good person is equally important too. When he comes home from school or from work, he looks at his family and remembers *Allah* who gifted him a place that is his sanctuary for love, care, and comfort. When he is well into old age, he remembers *Allah* and remembers that the gift of life is for him to understand what living is all about (and has he thought about it when he was much younger and full of idealism?). And when he is about to close his eyes for one last time, he remembers *Allah* who is going to deliver him into the next life that is more beautiful and everlasting than the present one he is having. Therefore, for a Muslim, *Allah* is a very significant presence in his life through which he understands his identity as a human being.

Thus, for a Muslim, *Allah* is always present with him. It appears that *Allah* is always in my life, thought, and activities. But most of all, it is *Allah* that my existence becomes a unity because in every moment of my life, in everything that I do, in whatever I may hope, I not only remember *Allah* but mention His name every now and then on my lips, having His name looming over my head when I am putting my thoughts into deeds, and adorning my home, garden, and room with beautiful calligraphies embellishing His name. Thus, for a Muslim, *Allah* is everything to him. Take away His name, and my identity means nothing.

In sum, *Allah* is the centre through which our view of the world is derived, our life organized, and our cultural expressions realized.

The Muslim life therefore is a life of God or Godly life as God is inseparable from any moment I am in or any activity I am engaged with or any situation I find myself in.

3

A Life with a Centre

The centre is the principle of everything. The centre holds everything at the edge together, without which, everything collapses. The centre is the principle of identity where everything knows what it means to exist and to be. The centre is the principle of relationship through which everything knows their place, position, and function in relation to the centre and in relation to everything else. The centre is the principle of action and movement where everything knows what to and what not to do in relation to one another. The centre, in short, is the source, guideline, and organization of whatever there is.

The centre and its edge is thus a helpful symbol to visualize one's identity as a human and a Muslim, a useful paradigm to measure one's relation to others, an effective model in prioritizing human actions, and a geometric model to construct cultural meanings of spatial designs, home decorations, as well as arts and crafts. The centre and its edge, in short, is like the moon and its reflections that are scattered across the oceans, lakes, and rivers.

Since God is the centre of everything, He is inevitably the source, principle and reference point through which we humans know what it means to exist and to be a human being. The *masjid* or mosque, namely, the Muslim house of worship, which represents the most important dimension of place, time and activity in the Muslim life, is the symbolic expression of the centrality of God in the Muslim life and through it, the Muslim imagines the centrality of God in his life and from which he relates to everything else through the mosque as his medium of connection from God to other things.

The mosque is the centre of space, time, and life of the Muslim community, but its physical appearance is not necessarily located in the middle of the living quarters of the Muslim residents. Rather, the centrality of the mosque in relation to its Muslim population lies more in its meaning than in its physical form. The mosque can be located in a faraway corner of a place, and yet it can still be imagined as the centre of everything around it.

The mosque is connected to all other places, from restaurants to schools to shops and even to washrooms, like the sun that shines on everything through its rays. The meaning that the mosque brings to a person is equally applied to other places. Thus, when a person walks out of a mosque and steps into a restaurant, or a shop, or a school, or a washroom, that person brings with him the meaning of the mosque and extends it into these other places. This way, his connection to God and religion is a continuous and an unbreakable one, from one place to another, from one environment to another and, from one condition to another.

God is bless and bliss and therefore life is also bless and bliss. A life of bless and bliss is a life of goodness because God is good and wishes good things to happen to human beings. The mosque, being the house of God, is the meeting point between man and God in its most focused condition where God's goodness flows into the worshipper's mind, heart, and body and through which his remembrance of God occurs most intensely, namely, his remembrance of God regarding His goodness to the life he enjoys having. As he steps out of the mosque and steps into a restaurant, his remembrance of God is extended into the restaurant he steps into, and he remembers God by remembering that goodness to life is the purpose of living.

In the restaurant, the person remembers God by reminding himself that the food he consumes is God's gift of life to him. He is grateful to God for the food without which, his body will be deprived of the nourishment that it so dearly needs. He is thankful to God because he knows that God loves him and is ever watching over his sustenance. The person therefore knows that God wishes the best for his health and well-being. He will avoid consuming food that could be harmful to his body, and be mindful to avoid wastage of food or consuming food in the like of gluttony.

A life of Islam is a life centred on *Allah* as the point for the blossoming of one's identity as a human being and through which he carries out that identity in all aspects of living, from thought to activity to expression of feeling, for Islam shines through everything from a centre where the light emanates and it is none other than the light of the sublime and the divine, that is to say, the light of God, Most Gracious, Most Merciful.

4

A Life of Purpose

A life in *Allah* is surely not a life of a wandering person with no idea of where he is going and heading. Rather, it is a life of purpose because one's life is like a string attached to a centre that directs and navigates his movements.

Life has four purposes—to become a *khalifah*, to do *ibadah*, to carry out *amal salih*, and to spread *isti'mar*.

Why did *Allah* bring us into existence, give us life, and then take us back to Him after a certain length of time on earth?

Earth is for us have a little taste of what life is so that when we have a taste of it, we would then know what it is to have it forever. But what is it that will motivate us to desire for a life of eternity, forever and ever? It is basically to realize our human accomplishment, that is to say, to become a human being in the noblest of meaning, namely, one who is knowledgeable and wise, who is loving, caring, and sharing, who is truthful, righteous and virtuous, and one who is artistic and beautiful. All of us should strive to realize these four aspects of our humanity that would make us into a person with a quality personality, called *khalifah*.

What is *khalifah* or vicegerent? *Khalifah* or vicegerent is one who has been given the honour, privilege and trust to transform earth that is filled with the dense jungles and dry deserts into a garden of delight and as we desire to make the world a paradise on earth, turning settlements into civilizations, we also make ourselves into human beings of the finest character, one who is good, righteous, wise, and beautiful, echoing what Prophet Muhammad said of his prophetic mission that 'Surely I was sent to bring into fruition and perfection those noble qualities of human character.'

In short, a *khalifah* is one who lives in true harmony and at peace with the transcendent and immanent, with God and the world, with other humans and himself, such that 'I am what I am because of who we all are.'

◆

Life's purpose then is to become a *khalifah*, and for us to be a *khalifah*, we need to do *ibadah*, that is to say, the worship of *Allah*.

The Qur'an is very clear on these two aims of life as it says, 'I (*Allah*) am to bring on earth a *khalifah* or vicegerent (Q2:30)' and 'I have not created the jinn and the humankind except that they should worship Me (Q51:56)'.

We should consider ourselves very honoured and privileged to be given earth for us to make it a wonderful place to live notwithstanding the fact that despite the gift of the intellect or mind, we have plenty of shortcomings that as we are able to construct a civilization from almost nothing, we are also able to destruct a civilization to almost nothing. We have the tendency to cause casualty to our very own humanity through quarrels over power, wealth, and glory. And yet, despite our tendency to turn the world upside down and wreak havoc to its inhabitants, we still find ourselves in the good book of God. And why so?

It is because we have another aspect of our creation and it is to do *ibadah*, to worship *Allah*, for in worshipping Him, we will be able to realize our status as *khalifah* in the full sense of its meaning. With *ibadah*, we will be guided in our behaviour about how we go about governing earth in true fashion according to the way of heaven as it is shown through divine revelation and prophetic mission that guide the intellect in putting heavenly words into earthly actions rather than be swayed by whims and fancies, passions and desires, just because we want to advance our dreams and ambitions. But what is *ibadah*, worshipping *Allah*?

◆

To some of us, mention the word worship and what comes to mind is a place where people go and offer their prayers such as the mosque, church, or temple.

For Muslims, worship has a wider meaning. To do the prayer (called *solat* in Islam) is an act of worship but to sleep, eat, play, and work are also acts of worship. The mosque is a place of worship but the school, bank, restaurant and stadium are also places where worship is carried out. To be with God, with *Allah* in prayer is worship but to be with family members, friends, and peers is also worship. Worship, for a Muslim, is a relationship that a person carries out with *Allah* which is then extended into his relationship with all that is in the world he lives in, from people to places to plants and animals.

When we say that the restaurant is a place of worship inasmuch as a mosque is, we do not mean that the restaurant is a place where we perform the prayer like how it is done in the mosque (in Malaysia, many shopping malls and petrol stations as well as Muslim restaurants have a prayer room for Muslims to pray). What this means is that the restaurant is a place where we carry out our meals' activities in accordance with the spirit of Islam, such as with regard to the way we behave at the table, about how we keep the table clean and tidy as well as not wasting the food we eat.

In Malaysia, most Western-style fast food eateries such as KFC and McDonald's serve only *halal* food i.e. food served according to the Islamic dietary laws, and this itself already makes these eateries Islamic in nature and a 'place of worship' insofar as the Muslims are concerned although the names may sound Western and the food have little relevance to the traditional Muslim cuisine. And, to make these eateries worthy as places of worship, these eateries practise quality control of the food they sell, practise good relationship with customers in terms of delivery and promptness, practise hygiene and cleanliness of the eateries, provide convenience for parents and children such as having a playground for the little ones, as well as other services which together sum up what worship is all about, that is, to establish a relationship with God where life is to produce a fine human character that enables a person to establish good relationships with his surrounding such that the places he goes to and the people he meets feel the serenity of his presence, like what the Prophet said that 'A Muslim is one whom others feel serene of his tongue and hand (what he says and does).'

Thus, the very purpose of human creation which is to be *Allah's khalifah* on earth can be realized to its full potential only if we try to accomplish it in the embrace of *ibadah*.

◆

By being a *khalifah* and the doing of *ibadah*, this will bring about the realization of a lofty humanity and personality, a transformation of places and people, and the attainment of quality living and cultured society which will eventually bring about the emergence of civilized people who will make this world a paradise on earth. This is called *isti'mar* or prospering. And like what the Qur'an says, 'He (*Allah*) has raised you from the earth and thereafter prospered you (*ista'mara-kum*) in it' (Q11:61).'

But in order to prosper, we need to commit to doing good, doing right, and doing proper. This is called *amal salih*. Without the right, good, and proper conduct of life, we can never enjoy a life of bless and bliss which in turn, will allow us to possess a culture of high manners, ethics, and etiquette, and eventually the attainment of a civilization adorned with fine works of arts and sciences that is the product of discipline, diligence, and commitment to producing human beings of the finest quality that the angels and even the devils cannot but admit that human beings are the worthy inheritors of earth to live and to govern, befitting their status as *khalifah*.

5

Life as *Khalifah*

*W*hat is a Muslim? A Muslim is not merely one who is defined as a person who embraces Islam as his religion. The more important question is—how, as a Muslim, I am a human being in the true sense of its meaning? To be a Muslim is not only to have a religion different from other religions but it is to have a religion through which the meaning, practising, and being human become realized. How is one a reflection of the ideal human being through becoming an ideal Muslim?

First and foremost, for a Muslim, his purpose of existence is to realize his identity as *khalifah*, or vicegerent, of *Allah* on earth. But what is *khalifah*?

'When your Lord said to the angels: 'I am to make on earth a *khalifah*, a vicegerent,' the angels said: 'Are you to make (on earth) one who is going to do mischiefs and shed blood, while we (the angels) adore and glorify You with praises and chant Your sacredness and holiness?' (And to which *Allah* replies), 'Surely I know what you (angels) know not (about this species called human) (Q2: 30)'.

The angels are a species of creation that are fully obedient to their creator and carry out His instructions without question. Thus, when they were told that there would be another species that would carry the mantle of leadership on earth but one that would commit mischief and fight one another, they were alarmed, and perhaps were offering themselves as a better alternative but were then told that their knowledge of this species, namely, human beings, is quite limited and therefore should leave the matter to the wisdom of their Lord.

To show that human beings know what the angels do not that would make them worthy inheritors of earth, *Allah* asked Adam to demonstrate his knowledge. 'And He i.e. *Allah* taught Adam (Adam is the first of the human species, the first human being on earth, the first Prophet of Islam, and the first *khalifah*) the names of all things and thereafter turned towards the angels and said, 'Tell me the names of these if you are indeed bearers of truth,' (and to which the angels replied), 'Glory be to You! We have no knowledge except what You taught us, for indeed You are most knowledgeable, most wise (Q2:31-32).'

Thus, what is it that Adam and his progeny knew that the angels do not that qualifies them to become God's vicegerents on earth?

◆

When *Allah* asks the angels to tell Him 'the names of these' and the angels could not do so, it could be that the angels possess only half of what humans could know, and it is that the angels know only the higher forms of knowledge that are perfect, complete, and ones that breed obedience and submission, but not the knowledge of the other half that pertains to incompleteness and imperfection, knowledge that is required for one to inhabit and govern earth, knowledge of a kind where we must move from insufficiency to sufficiency such that along the way, we move from individuality to collectivity and finally to embrace the whole of everything where everything is none other than the divine names and attributes of *Allah* that are spread across the universe and manifesting as *ayat* or signs intended for us to make sense of our purpose in this world and for us to govern earth in line with the purpose of our creation, which is to realize our status as *khalifah* as a human being called a Muslim, one who understands what it is to know the 'names of everything' that *Allah* has taught him.

Mankind has shown that they possess a mind that with it, is able to make them into creatures of a different kind from the rest of others, but despite the prowess of the mind, they possess the tendency to lapse into forgetfulness about their true nature as a species of insufficiency and as a result, are overwhelmed by the false impression that they are great, strong, and self-sufficient that they need no other than themselves to make the world an empire of living.

But no sooner do they think they could build a haven of living on earth, they found that they were going at each other's throat in pursuit of their personal insatiable desires for want of more gains compared to others, and, as a consequence, brought wrath upon themselves for their self-interest, self-centredness, selfishness, ego-centrism, haughtiness, and proud-ness. These destructive elements of the self are caused by the failure to recognize that inasmuch as our intelligence brings us a world of wonders for living, we still need to rely on a far greater source to guide our intelligence to make the world a sanctuary for the realization of the truly human being.

It is therefore pertinent for us humans to know that our intelligence is not only to realize that we could be sufficient, but more importantly, it is for us to realize that we are insufficient in the first place, and, to be sufficient, we have to commit to a higher source of intelligence that will make our own intelligence something that brings not only the material comfort of life but also makes us into becoming human beings of the most noble kind, creatures that are filled not only with knowledge but also with wisdom, love, virtue, sympathy, empathy, mercy, and compassion, for others inasmuch as it is for one's own self.

This 'higher intelligence' is none other than God and through the guidance that He provides for mankind, called *wahy* or revelation, it awakens mankind from their forgetfulness about their mission on earth.

◆

It is forgetfulness that causes mankind to lose sight of the higher level of knowledge and leaves them with the lower level of knowledge. As such, guidance coming from heaven becomes necessary for in the absence of divine guidance, mankind is left with knowledge of the worldly life that could plunge them into conflicts with one another but with guidance coming from *Allah*, their knowledge of the worldly life is guided by the knowledge about how the worldly life should be pursued and lived, so that through knowing what it is to be insufficient and rebellious, they know how to become dependent and obedient.

It is because human beings know that they are insufficient that they can know the deeper and more profound meaning of such things like caring, sharing, togetherness, and belongingness, precious values of humanity that could only be realized if these are cultivated together by all of us who are called humans through a centre of guidance coming from heaven.

Thus, while the angels know what it is to be a creature in all respects of its sufficiency, they do not have the necessary knowledge about what it is to be insufficient. They thought that the insufficiencies that human beings have could not make them good governors of earth, but they did not know that it is the insufficiencies that would make humans good governors on earth.

Needless to say, what appears as a weakness to the angels is in fact a strength that would enable human beings to assume the mantle of leadership on earth but with the condition that they hold on firmly to the guidance of heaven that would steer their weakness into becoming their strength and consequently their rightful place as *khalifah* on earth.

6

A Life of Worship

For many of us today, when we think of worship, what immediately comes to mind is the scene of people praying at holy places, such as the mosque, church, or temple.

Worship, it seems, is a time to seek forgiveness and to atone for one's misdoings, a time to seek strength against the many adversities that one is facing, a time to seek consolation for one's worries, and a time to seek approval and blessings for life's sanctity. Worship then, is a relationship with a sacred character for the procurement of things that bring about good consequences to one's life and living.

For Muslims, worship extends beyond the mosque. The mosque serves as a connecting point between what is done inside and what is done outside it.

Praying is worship but so is eating and drinking, washing and cleaning oneself, taking care of plants and flowers, playing football and swimming, watching TV, and even sleeping. As long as the activities we do are meant to keep us healthy, become knowledgeable persons and upright in our human conduct, be polished in our manners and etiquette of speaking, writing, and interacting, and all those fine things of human living, these are considered as worship in Islam.

As such, worship is not only specific acts done in specific places and at specific times. Worship is all the time, at all places and involves every single act and activity.

◆

The word to denote worship is *ibadah*. For something to be considered *ibadah*, a person has to intend the thing for the sake of *Allah*. This is the *niyyah* or intention. Then one has to do it for the thing's sake. This is sincerity or *ikhlas*. And, the thing has to bring about *maslaha* or goodness to the human life and also conforms to the sanctity of religion in terms of what's good or not, what's right or otherwise, and what's permissible or forbidden.

Therefore, to be considered *ibadah*, three conditions are required—(a) intention (b) sincerity and (c) goodness.

Planting flowers is considered *ibadah* when one makes the intention of filling one's home with lovely things so that one's surrounding would appear pleasant and beautiful, and this will remind oneself of the saying of Prophet Muhammad that '*Allah* is Beautiful and He loves beautiful things.' Thus, planting flowers to bring about a colourful environment would connect one to *Allah* through the element of beauty that when a person sees the beautiful flowers, he will immediately be full of praise for *Allah* who makes beautiful things to add splendour into our life.

Giving charity is a very noble deed and one who is charitable is a praiseworthy person because he is willing to share what he earns with the less privileged. To give charity or *sadaqah* is *ibadah* but to give charity so that one may be seen as charitable or be praised as a generous person is not doing it for the sake of generosity and charity and therefore his act is not regarded as *ibadah*. A person who is not sincere will not continue to give the moment he finds the heaps of praises for him are not forthcoming. He will feel dejected, disappointed and even angry that he is not credited for what he is doing. Thus, even though outwardly a thing may appear to be an act of *ibadah*, in reality, it is not *ibadah* because it is not made with the right intention and with sincerity, for the Prophet has said, 'Every act or deed issues forth from intention.'

Abu Hurairah narrated a *hadith* or saying of the Messenger of *Allah* about *riya'* or doing something for the sake of wanting to be seen. An example will be a wealthy man who will be brought before *Allah* who will say to him: 'Was I not so generous with you that I did not leave you without any need from anyone?' He will reply: 'Of course O Lord!' *Allah* will ask: 'Then what did you do with what I gave to you?' He will say: 'I would nurture the ties of kinship and give charity.' Then *Allah* will say to him: 'You have lied. Rather, you wanted it to be said that so-and-so is so generous, and that was said (meaning that you wanted to get appreciated and that's what happened).'

◆

It is therefore pertinent that we make ourselves continuously present in *ibadah* because by so doing, we can bring about the quality of truthfulness in ourselves, a quality that qualifies us to be a true human being, one who is what he is actually, not one who is a hypocrite, being someone in front of others and being someone else in front of some others. Regarding the hypocrite or *munafiq*, the Prophet said, 'The signs of the hypocrite are three—when he speaks he lies, when he promises he breaks his promise, and when he is entrusted he betrays the trust.' Similarly, a person who gives charity but his intention is not about the charity but is about promoting himself is a hypocrite.

Needless to say, hypocrisy is when what a thing appears as and what it really is are not the same.

Therefore, being in *ibadah* in the true sense of its meaning means that what a person projects himself outwardly, that is also what he is inwardly. *Ibadah* connects him with *Allah* and through this connection, he gets to synchronize and put his actions and his intentions together so that they are sincere, for the sake of what the thing is intended, and for the sake of *Allah*.

Therefore, in the fulfillment of our needs, wants, and desires, we must make sure these are pursued as *ibadah* at all times, in all situations, at all places, and with regard to all activities and actions so that we will become human beings who are truthful in our character, rightful in our conduct, and as a result, beautiful in our personality.

Worship at first glance appears to be everything about God but in reality, it is really about man and his becoming a noble human being. The more we are into God, the more noble our humanity becomes.

7

A Life of Prayer

Prophet Muhammad has said, 'Prayer or *solat* is the foundation by which religion is erected. Whosoever erects the prayer erects the religion. And whosoever derelicts the prayer derelicts the religion.' And the Prophet also said, 'The first thing to be queried on the Day of Judgment is the prayer.' The Prophet also said, 'The distinguishing mark between one who has God in his heart with one who neglects God in his life is the prayer.'

That the Prophet gives so much emphasis to the prayer says volume to its significance and importance in the Muslim life.

Prayer puts us in right perspectives of things, positions us in the proper relationship with everything, and points us to the preferred views in whatever we are thinking, doing and expressing.

◆

When we pray, the first thing we bear in mind is that God is the beginning and end of everything. As God is the point of departure and return, He is therefore the centre through which we derive our sense of existence.

With God, we come to know who we are, what life means, how we go about with our activities, how we relate to our surroundings and, after we die, where we will be heading. Prayer connects us to these essential questions of life when it connects us with God.

Knowing that God is the beginning of everything means knowing that God is the first of everything and comes first before everything. And knowing that God is the end of everything means knowing that when everything has passed out of existence, God is still there and does not perish. Or that when everything is said or done, God is there waiting for us to rest our hope in Him so that everything will turn out good and fine and as the saying goes, 'As man proposes, it is God who disposes.' Needless to say, as we begin a thing, God is there with us and, after we finish a thing, God is there waiting for us.

Prayer, in this connection, puts us in a position where we will realize the meaning of priority, about what comes first and what comes after, and why prioritizing helps us to understand relationships and actions better and how it will enhance our human dignity.

Prayer puts God nearest to us and us nearest to Him. In standing before God, we put God before everything else so that it is only Him that is the focal point of our mind and heart, the focus of our attention. When our mind and heart become aware of the overwhelming presence of God, we will feel the greatness of His presence and the smallness of our own existence.

In prayer, we come to know the significance of God to our existence. But to know that God is great is not to make us feel intimidated and hence, helpless, but it is to make us know that in whatever we do, we should not assume that we know everything and can do anything and therefore can have full control over our destiny as well as the outcome of things. Such an attitude will only breed overconfidence and eventually self-pride, haughtiness, and egoism to the extent that we can end up becoming a person who sees only me as the reason and cause for the success of everything. But with God, this attitude is broken and instead we will see ourselves as only a part of a larger picture of existence, a little piece of a jigsaw puzzle that participates to make things happen which requires others too to come in and help build the whole picture of life.

With God, we learn about insufficiency and inadequacy and why we need others and others need us to make a complete picture of things. With God, we learn about the meaningfulness of dependence so that we can come to be an active participant along with our other fellow humans to make life happens. With God, we learn what it is to be humble and not arrogant. We learn what it is to be human. Prayer, in this respect, helps us to remember God and in remembering God, we remember who we are as a creature called human. But what is remembrance of God about?

◆

In remembering God, we remember that God is the source of

our existence and therefore our light of guidance, the light that illuminates our mind and heart so that we could see the path of our human life—what we have intended, what we have spoken, what we have done, and what we have accumulated for our livelihood.

We reflect upon these things, and ask ourselves, 'Was I sincere in my intentions? Have I spoken things that may have caused grievances to others? Have I done things that may have brought negative consequences upon my own self and upon others? Have I been honest in the accumulation of the things for my livelihood? Have I been neglectful of the good that I must and should do?'

Remembrance of God is thus a key connection between us and God. Remembrance of God will motivate and move us into seeking Him for constant guidance and reminders. We seek Him for answers, for assurance of life, for direction, for sustenance, for security, for solace, for our well-being in this world and for a life of bless and bliss. 'And seek Him with patience and prayer, surely these appear burdensome for the heavy-hearted except those who are constantly devoted in the remembrance of God (Q2:45)'.

From prayer, the remembrance of God is extended into our thoughts, feelings, and activities, like a drop of water that would cause its surrounding to ripple out from its centre.

◆

Muslims pray five times a day, from dawn till dusk, before the sun is up and after the sun goes down, and each time a person finishes one prayer, another one awaits him. This would appear as if there is nothing else to do in life except to pray, and questions will be flying abound as to what kind of life a person is having that is so filled with one prayer after another.

Between one prayer and another, a person will be attending to his everyday needs, such as work, play, eat and drink and all those necessary things of everyday living.

As he finishes his prayer and attends to his other needs, he brings prayer into these other things of everyday living, connecting what he says and does in his prayer to what he says and does outside it.

In this sense, prayer connects to other aspects and activities of life. Take drinking coffee for instance. Many of us drink coffee for all kinds of reasons. We drink coffee to quench our thirst, or for the taste that we find pleasant, or for the warmth that coffee does to our body, or to keep the eyes awake so that we don't fall asleep while driving! But in drinking coffee (and other drinks for that matter) a person reminds himself that any drink that he takes must not be harmful or detrimental to his body, mind, and health, one that will affect his thoughts, movements, and activities, such as causing drunkenness.

As such, between one prayer and another, the Muslim is kept firmly on his toe about what he has done and is going to do, and the consequences following from his deeds or actions, whether regarding what he intends, says, or does. When he finishes one prayer, he ponders over his deeds and actions and reflects on them, and asks if they have been praiseworthy and likeable or, on the contrary, blameworthy and undesirable. But more importantly, he asks how he shall face God when he enters prayer the next time? How would his conscience feel, and react, for what he has intended, said, or done?

It is no wonder that the Qur'an underscores the importance and significance of the *solat* to our life, by saying, 'Certainly prayer guides (us) away from *fahshah* i.e. shameful acts and *munkar* i.e. degrading conducts (Q29:45)'.

As such, prayer is not only an act of worship that is done because it is a command, but because in doing it, the meaning of our humanity is brought out into the surface of our psychology and extends into our ethics as well as our interactions with our fellow humans and, of course, with the birds and beasts, rivers and streams, flowers and trees, that is to say, with all that is part of our human unity.

8

A Life of Purity

$\mathscr{A}$ life of Islam is a life that emphasizes purity as its basis of living. Purity is not only with regard to cleanliness of place, food, and clothes, but also with regard to sanctity of faith, thought, and action.

Therefore, for one to be properly called a Muslim, he must understand the meaning and place of purity in the life of a Muslim without which he cannot expect good things to come out from his heart, mind, and behaviour.

Life, through many of the things we see, touch, and feel, needs to be refreshed every now and then. We human beings are always excited at getting new things, as new things are refreshing, lift our spirit, arouse our excitement, reinvigorate our energy, and, tomorrow will be quite a welcoming day to start our life again.

For those of us having cars, for instance, we will send the cars for washing and polishing so that the cars will look new and shiny and we will then have a better mood to drive. For those of us who have a home, we do not like our home to look the same all the time, and we would try to change the look of our home's interior, get it repainted, or even renovated. A refreshing look makes us dwell and sleep well.

In the same way, renewing and refreshing life, in whatever we do, will make us a new and refreshed person, today, tomorrow, and every single day.

For a Muslim, to renew and refresh life is to enable him to have a life of purity. Purity, for a Muslim, is to purge one's self from all the filth that has gathered in one's soul that, if not attended to, could cause him to do things that may not be pleasant in the eyes of others. After all, we do send our cars and computers for servicing so that they will continue to enjoy a longer lifespan. In the same way, we need to get ourselves 'serviced' so that we could continue to have a pleasant life, and a pleasant life means being pleasant in one's conduct of life, towards one's self and also towards others.

◆

Purification comes in five forms. The first is the most common to all of us and it is the cleanliness of our surrounding and environment so that we could have a comfortable place to live, such as having the air we breathe free from pollution and the water free from contamination, rid our homes of pests and insects and the weeds growing everywhere, and getting our body and clothes cleansed from all the mud and dirt that cause filth and plenty of discomfort. All these are purification in the physical sense. It is called *nazafah*, and like what the Prophet said, 'Nazafah, cleanliness, is part of iman, part of one's religious life.'

The second type of purification is with regard to the acquisition and consumption of the means of livelihood, such as money, food, and even services. This is called halal and toyyib, or permissible and good. It is no point for one to live a life that is mired in ill-gotten gains because whatever he consumes from these gains will turn into his flesh and blood and how could one expect good to come to his soul if his body is tainted with unjust means of livelihood? Therefore it is important that our livelihood is acquired through halal means and is of toyyib quality, namely, through the proper channel of acquisition that will ensure the purity of our consumption and the good consequences upon our health and wealth.

The third type of purification is to purge our thoughts, feelings and desires from all the blameworthy elements, elements that could cause us to become human beings with a base character that nobody wants to come near, elements such as envy, hate, jealousy, pride, selfishness, and actions such as lying, cheating, practising corruption, and so on. It is also to purge ourselves from words coming out from the tongue and the tendency to slur, curse, backbite, and even say filthy words. It is also with regard to what we hear such as hearsays, gossips that are blameworthy in nature, and fitnah or slanderous accusations. And it is also with regard to what we see, namely, material that would incite to lust and passion such as pornography and X-rated films, for instance. This type of purification is called tazkiyyah.

The fourth type of purification is taharah or cleansing one's body according to the prescription of religion, such as how one cleanses one's self after going to toilet or how one makes the *wudu'* before doing the *solat* or prayer.

The fifth type of purification is called *tawhid,* namely, to keep one's attachment to *Allah* pure from all kinds of misunderstanding of His nature as God.

◆

Seen together, all five forms of purification are connected to one another. A person who is not bothered with the cleanliness of his surrounding, or his home, or even his own body, is a person who cannot be bothered with the responsibility and respect towards self, others, and God.

On the contrary, a person who is conscious and conscientious about his own self will do all that is necessary to make himself physically healthy, morally responsible, and spiritually enlightened and these can only be achieved if he takes care of his body, thoughts, and behaviour from falling into decadence and becoming insipid. If his body and soul become decadent and insipid, his life will turn from one that is vibrant and buoyant into one that is listless and cheerless that, in the end, will produce a person who is not bothered with himself as well as with his fellow humans, the ecology, and all that is sacred and holy.

Impurity, or *najasah,* is an impediment to human growth, social coherence, ecological well-being, and spiritual enlightenment and to prevent impurity from causing decadence in our soul and disrupting our psychology that will turn us into an undesirable personality , we need to make sure that purity, in its five forms, must be cultivated, pursued, practised, maintained, and improved at all times, day and night, morning and evening, and every second of our everyday living, right from the moment we open our eyes until the moment we close our eyes for one last time. Only then can serenity and equanimity seep into our soul and from there, flow out to form a harmony of heaven, earth, and human and with it, a unity of existence between God, ecology, and man.

9

A Life of Virtue

Prophets did not emerge in the midst of the human race to teach them about the arts and sciences of constructing buildings and canals. These skills came together when men appeared on earth. Rather, Prophets were sent to instruct men on the skills of proper living, that in building life on earth, there are guidelines to follow so that as they construct a beautiful life to savour, they do not destroy it altogether.

We humans are a strange lot. Inasmuch as we toil and sweat to build a wonderful life to live, we also have the tendency to decimate the things essential for our living. And this is because we forgot that I am what I am because of who we all are, that we are a family of togetherness in existence, and that I am an individual who need others to define my identity as a human being. And, for that, the very reason that Prophets were sent was to teach us about how to become a good human being and not only a useful human being.

As human beings, we need to be both useful and good. The absence of one will not contribute to the overall well-being of the human personality. However, we humans were already endowed with the ability to be useful as witnessed in human history. We have shown that we are able to transform the dense jungles into places filled with skyscrapers and the dry deserts into green pastures. With only a little brain lodged in the head, we are able to bring the whole world to our feet with our ideas as well as our creativity.

But again and again, we also witness in human history how we are ready to destroy lives and properties. The scale of destruction of human lives in the two world wars in the 20th century is testimony to what we humans are capable of doing, indeed a very scary testimony of how destructive we humans can become.

Therefore, the task of the Prophets is to guide us into channelling our brain and brawn for the betterment of the human race, that inasmuch as we can be useful in our ability to construct, we too must be good in our conduct.

Knowing how to produce more food is a useful venture of the brain but producing food through genetic engineering that causes harm to the body for the purpose of profit making is surely not a good thing.

Goodness springs from the heart. There was a story about how someone came to a poison maker and asked him to make him poison of the most deadly kind. After the poison was ready, this someone asked the poison maker if there was anything more poisonous than the poison that he made. The poison maker said 'yes.' This someone was startled and asked what that could be and the poison maker said, 'The human heart.'

◆

The human heart is the most important part of our human personality so that Prophet Muhammad would say, 'In the body is a piece of flesh. If it is good then the whole body too will be good. If it is corrupt then the whole body will be corrupt. This is the heart.'

The heart is the connecting point between what is physical and spiritual, between human and divine, between us and God. It has an aspect called conscience. Conscience is such that when we do or think of doing something wrong, an inner voice will call out to us and tell us that it is not a right thing to do and we will be overcome by guilt and shame. A father who steals knows that stealing is a wrong thing to do and he will advise his children not to do it even though he himself does it. This is because his conscience knocks sense into his soul and tells him that stealing is a very wrong thing to do.

If we do not take care of our conscience and our heart, our soul will gradually be overtaken by the tendency to commit blameworthy things to the extent that we will no longer feel guilty or ashamed of doing them.

Therefore it is important that from the day we were born, we receive proper guidance about how we take care of our soul so that as we grow to become useful persons, we also grow with goodness spreads and reverberates all over our mind, body and behaviour that, in the end, will produce a personality in us that befits our status as *khalifah* on earth.

10

A Life of Sincerity

The most precious thing about being human is that we shall be worthy to be called a human being. And, one of the most precious things that would make us worthy to be called a human being is sincerity or *ikhlas*. In fact, sincerity is one of the fundamental virtues that by it, we blossom into a human being of the finest kind.

To be a Muslim is to be a sincere human being. That is what becoming a Muslim is, namely, that we become a person who is truthful with what we say, and be truthful with what we do. We do not deceive ourselves and others.

Sincerity is to be what we are, and not that we pretend to be what we are not. Sincerity is to do what we are supposed to do, and not because of some other motives. Sincerity is to know that in whatever we become and in whatever we do, we acknowledge others in our achievements, and not that we turn a blind eye on them and take all the credit for our accomplishments even if we think it is we who made all the efforts that contributed to our successes.

However, to be sincere is not an easy thing to do as we are always getting distracted by elements that would detach us from our efforts to be sincere. And worse, not only will we be detached from these efforts, we can be pulled away from them that, in the end, we would rather abandon these efforts and instead be immersed in all the satisfaction of having our ego inflated because being bigger than what you are can make you feel proud and worthy.

But the nightmare begins once we are able to see how insincerity will lead us to the path of destruction because we will say things that we don't know but think we know and do things that we think will give the desired results but instead give the opposite outcomes.

We are creatures who easily forget, and easily succumb to praises, and, as a result, we end up imagining things about ourselves that sometimes are not what we are. In the same way, we don't like being criticized or be shown to have weaknesses because we would be seen as lacking in our personality and ability. We prefer to be seen as perfect and have no defects!

When our mind and heart are swarmed with the disillusionment that we are always perfect and devoid of defects, what follows are the negative and blameworthy elements emerging in our soul.

◆

The first of these destructive elements is egoism or *takabbur*. Egoism is the chief element that breeds all the other destructive elements. Egoism is where we think highly of ourselves and think petty of others.

Egoism breeds haughtiness, self-pride, and narcissism where we see only ourselves as worthy of regard, attention, and praise and others are not worthy of anything. Thus, when we are asked to carry out a group task, for example, and thereafter achieved a good result, we would try to show that we are the one behind the success of the task, such as boasting about our ability and thinking to ourselves that if it is not because of me, the desired result would not have been achieved. And not only that, we will try to ignore the contribution of others in the group and will try not to speak about them with regard to their performance. Worse, we may even go to the extent of manipulating and abusing others to advance our own interest or ambition. This is called *'ujub* or obsession with one's own self, namely, self-centredness, self-pride and selfishness.

'Ujub can lead to the silent or hidden act of associating oneself with the power of God or *shirk khafi*. A person of ego thinks that he is the reason why things become what they are. He thinks he has some kind of power that could make things happen, or even possesses some kind of aura that could get people to be glued to his words as if his words are some kind of mantra able to turn these people into his followers.

For such a person who thinks his words are mantra and his acts are magic, he cannot but must seek public attention and recognition, and for that, he needs to show off his knowledge, skill, and ability. This is called *riya'* or wanting to be seen.

Riya' is a very clear and manifest sign of insincerity because the person will show his pretensions or make promises to do this and that in front of people but the moment they come forward to seek his promises, he will backtrack on his words, or worse, vanish without a trace. He follows where attention takes him and treats those who come to him for help as a menace and a burden as well as a hindrance to his popularity-seeking trade.

A person of *riya'* is not likely to be trusted of his words as he will not likely honour them because he made them not with the intention of fulfilling them but with the intention of seeking self-recognition, attention and popularity. This is called hypocrisy, namely, *nifaq* or *munafiq*. His words are sweet talks and his actions are nothing but empty promises. Because the heart is already filled with hypocrisy, *hasad* or envy will govern his soul and be his watchdog to see if there is any attempt to take away his egoism. He cannot see others being given due recognition of their knowledge, skill, ability, or contribution, or be seen as being better than his personality or doing better than what he is doing. His heart will be lurking with all kinds of hatred and jealousy and his mind will be scheming with all kinds of ill-intents about how to belittle or even bring down those who are being and doing better than him.

As a result, egoism that breeds all the destructive elements in the soul will also bring about all the destructive acts in a person. Lying, exaggerating, boasting, and misleading are some of the conspicuous destructive acts of the tongue. Ignorance, superficiality, and stupidity are some of the acts of the mind when a person speaks his thoughts and ideas. His behaviour as well as his work will be meant with the aim to impress but nothing to express his ability and depth of knowledge.

Needless to say, a person of such nature who is insincere from head to toe is akin to one who masters the techniques of courtship and is able to sweet talk and dazzle a girl into believing his charming appearance as well as his promises, but when it comes to the actual marriage, he fails as a husband because he does not have what it takes to be someone who could be responsible or is dedicated to his marriage life as it requires a lot of patience, understanding and overcoming differences and weaknesses to make the marriage work. And most importantly, it requires him to forego his ego in order to let his spouse become part of his life and have a say in whatever he thinks and does.

◆

The *fardhu ain* i.e. the necessary things for everyday living are there to help us cope with the problem of egoism and turn us in the direction of becoming the kind of person worthy to be called a human being.

Through the *fardhu ain,* we will find ourselves always in touch with *Allah,* from the moment we wake up from sleep until the moment we go to bed. The *du'a,* for instance, is one way that keeps us in touch with *Allah. Du'a* is beseeching or asking for *Allah*'s help or favour.

When we open our eyes after a good night's sleep, we will immediately realize that we are given another chance at life. We therefore give thanks to *Allah* for the life He continues giving us but at the same time ask ourselves how we are going to behave with a new day given to us. That is why it is important for us to read the *du'a* that says '*Allahumma a'inni 'ala zikri-ka wa syukri-ka wa husni 'ibadahti-ka,*' meaning, 'O *Allah*. Fortify me with the remembrance of You, being thankful to You, and to carry out my life's activities in the best of quality.'

This *du'a* contains three significant things that will keep our ego in check. These are *zikr*, *syukr*, and *husn ibadah*.

Zikr is mindfulness as well as remembrance of *Allah*. A person who is mindful of *Allah* is a person who knows that behind everything there stands *Allah* as the real cause of what we possess and what we accomplish. This is not to say that our part in whatever we do is overlooked or obliterated so that God takes credit for all that we achieve, but it is to remind us that our achievements are not because of our own efforts alone. We may put in all the efforts to make a thing happen, but whether it happens according to how we want it and whether we have full control over it, sometimes this is beyond our ability to decide its outcome and destiny.

Needless to say, things do not always happen according to plan although we try to make sure that they go according to plan. Doctors, for instance, can tell us that even with years of knowledge and experience and with the availability of the most advanced equipment to help save lives, they cannot guarantee one hundred percent the diseases they treat can be cured fully or the life of a patient can be saved for sure. The most the doctors can give is the degree of probability, namely, what are the chances for the cure or the survival and what they can do to get the best result from their treatment.

That there are limits to our knowledge and ability is

perhaps one way that *Allah* wants us to be aware of our insufficiencies and shortcomings, that we must never go overboard with the belief that we can know everything and can do anything. On the contrary, we will always look to Him to measure our beliefs and actions so that as we put in the knowledge and efforts in order to make a thing work, we also put the trust and hope in *Allah* that He will give the best outcome for what we think and do.

In this regard, a Muslim always says *'Bismillah, tawakkaltu 'ala Allah'* meaning, 'In the name of *Allah*, in Him I rest my trust and hope.' This is called *tawakkul*. After all, He is God and although we humans do participate, for instance, to produce food to eat that comes in all kinds of names and tastes, it is God who provides the seed, the soil, and the water for the food to grow and for us to savour it. Therefore, a Muslim is one who is always mindful that behind all that we know and all that we do, there stands *Allah* who gifted life for us to enjoy, supplies us with all the basic necessities to build a life, and endowed us with a mind that will brim with knowledge for us to make life a reality filled with joy.

◆

A person who is mindful is a person who is grateful. This is called *syukr* or being thankful. A person who is mindful is a person who pays attention to what he sees, thinks, and does. When he sees food in front of him, he is mindful that it is *Allah* who gifted him the food. He thanks *Allah* for the food he gets but in thanking *Allah* for the food, he is mindful that there are others who may not be as fortunate as him, and his mind will wander to these people, be sympathetic with their condition which in turn will alert him to his own condition so that he becomes more responsible towards his own well-being and at the same time makes him to be a humble person as well.

Being thankful therefore stretches a person's sense of love and care for his own self into loving and caring for others because as he feels thankful or grateful, he doesn't only think of himself but makes others a part of him as well.

To care and have sympathy for others, we must first begin with taking care and be sympathetic to our own condition. If we are a parent, we want to make sure that our children do not consume things that will bring harm to them, with regard to what they eat and drink and with regard to what they see. We surely do not wish our children to drink alcoholic drinks as well as smoke cigarettes, nor do we wish to see them watch pornographic material that will affect their sexual behaviour towards themselves as well as others.

If we do not wish our children to develop into the kind of human being who will be problematic with his health, thought, and behaviour, then we ourselves must make sure we do not do the things that we do not want our children to do. All good things must therefore begin with us before they can happen with others.

◆

It is in being mindful and grateful to *Allah* that we find our everyday living a *husn ibadah*, namely, our actions will be those that bring only praiseworthy consequences to self and others as we are constantly under the shadow of mindfulness and gratefulness as we undertake to discharge our actions.

A life of Islam is a life of sincerity. Sincerity will make us truthful and honest, mindful and careful, loving and caring, and at the same time take away self-centredness, arrogance, and pretension from looming in our soul. It is therefore pertinent to lead a life of sincerity so that we shall become a human being that truly reflects the vision and mission of Islam for the meaning and purpose of being human.

11

A Life of Culture

For many of us, mention culture, and we tend to think of costumes, home decorations, songs and musical instruments, food and cooking, festivals, crafts, patterns and designs, dances, greetings and hospitality, and all those things that highlight the artistic tastes and aesthetical expressions of an ethnic group that would give it its unique ethnic identity.

For some of us, culture is the habits of a 'high society' as against a 'common society,' in manner of speaking, dressing, eating, writing, and interacting. It is also about which places we go for our lunch and dinner, what kinds of music we listen to, which type of persons we align and mix with, and so on and so forth. In this sense, a person of culture is some kind of 'human being of a higher degree' as he is able to acquire and exhibit the finer qualities of life's delight as opposed to the 'coarse' behaviour of persons such as farmers and labourers.

Edward Tylor, a 19th century British anthropologist, said

that culture is 'That complex whole which includes knowledge, belief, art, morals, law, custom, and any other capabilities and habits acquired by man as a member of society.'

Clifford Geertz, an American anthropologist of religion, points out that culture is not only about how people *do* things but also about how they *see* things. Culture is therefore a worldview and a set of values called ethos, that characterize the way a people express their beliefs, thoughts, and feelings. Geertz says, 'In anthropology, it has become customary to refer to the collection of notions a people has of how reality is at base put together as their worldview. Their general style of life, the way they do things and like to see things done, we usually call their ethos. It is the office of religious symbols (i.e. culture) then to link these in such a way that they mutually confirm one another. Such symbols (i.e. cultural expressions, forms, and practices) render the world believable because the ethos, which grows out of it, is felt to be authoritative; the ethos is justifiable because the worldview, upon which it rests, is held to be true.' He further states, 'It is the conviction that the values one holds are grounded in the inherent structure of reality, that between the way one ought to live and the way things really are there is an unbreakable connection. What sacred symbols do for those to whom they are sacred is to formulate an image of the world's construction and a program for human conduct that are mere reflexes of one another.'

Thus, culture acquires a variety of meanings. If taken together, it can be said that culture is *theoria, praxis*, and *poiesis*. It is about how we see things (*theoria*), how we do things (*praxis*), and what things we create and produce (*poiesis*). More specifically, it is about what we see in life that is meaningful to us that thrusts us into pursuing, upholding, and cherishing those values, outlooks, ideals, wishes, and dreams, so that what we produce, whether it is for the material or non-material fulfillment of life, becomes realized as items and patterns of living.

◆

Muslims call culture by a variety of names, such as *thaqafah*, *hadarah*, and *adab*. *Adab* is closely tied to literary achievements. Malay Muslims understand *adab* as manners, and in the traditional Malay society, to have *adab* is to know how to behave towards others in the proper way. Thus, it is considered an *adab* for children to kiss their parents' hands when greeting them, that one should give the *salam* before entering the house, that women should appear shy in public and put on a *selendang* or a long piece of cloth wrap over the head when going out.

For Syed Muhammad Naquib al-Attas, a contemporary scholar of Islamic thought and Malay studies, *adab* goes much deeper than just a show of talent and an expression of manners. Talent and manners spring from a more fundamental aspect of life, and it is education. For Attas, *adab* is acculturation or *ta'dib*, the incessant process of realizing the *tawhidic* self, namely, the self that blossoms from *Allah* for his human identity.

According to Attas, the loss of *adab* is the reason why Muslims in modern times have dwindled in their cultural attainments because they could no longer discern between priorities and sequences in knowledge and action, resulting in the loss of justice to their soul, self, person, vision, relationship, and interaction where justice is knowing how to put things in their proper position so that the proper consequences and implications could come about when things are put where they rightly belong. Thus, a person of *adab* is a person who not only knows the right order of things but also knows how to put things in the right order. God comes first in this order of priority, sequence, relationship, and action, followed by Prophet Muhammad, and thereafter the righteous leaders and the true persons of learning, the *umara'* and *ulama'* so to speak but of the genuine type. They (*i.e.* God, Prophet Muhammad, *umara', ulama'*) become the standard for the measurement of life, thought, and action, so that whatever we do as our cultural expressions and achievements, the consequences of these expressions and achievements must lead to the arrival of the *tawhidic* meaning into the soul that would then attune the mind, body, spirit, intentions, movements, communications, and interactions into a unity of existence— with self, others, environment, and the transcendent so that the person of Islam, called the Muslim, is the outcome of this process of acculturation.

This is the mark of a person of culture, of a Muslim who in his thoughts, feelings, doings, and aesthetic expressions, lead to the realization of the personality of *khalifah* in the preservation, promotion, and protection of humanity, in terms of his human identity, use of his mental ability, discharge of the property, respect of life's sanctity, well-being of the progeny, and upholding each other's dignity, whether in arts or activities, in ways of eating, dressing, working, gardening, drinking, learning, relaxing, interacting, celebrating, and all the things of everyday living.

12

A Life of Togetherness

$\mathcal{A}$ life of Islam is a life of togetherness. For many of us, when we think of ourselves, we tend to see ourselves as distinct individuals detached from the rest of us so that what we call I or me is someone who is independent from the rest of others.

To the contrary, as a human being, we are made up of four selves, namely 'me', then 'we' as a union of human beings, then 'us' as a larger union with the non-human living beings, and finally, I am 'all' that includes God as the source of my existence and that of others. Thus, when I see myself, I see me in all the four aspects of my identity, namely, a self that I consciously know that it is me (individual or personal self), a self in relation with others (relational self), a self that shares in common with others (collective self), and a self that has a higher degree of existence (transcendent self).

When I look at myself, I am aware that I am different and

yet I sense resemblance and similarity with my fellow humans. I also sense that I have affinity with the wonderful world of Nature which I inhabit, namely, the skies and seas, forests and greeneries, birds and bees. And, I also know that, as I look at whatever is around me, I sense a blessed and sacred world that I live in and, wherever I may be, God is there for me.

Therefore, the first thing about my human meaning is that everything, from me to my fellow humans to the rivers and fishes and to whatever beyond this little world, is all part of me.

◆

Although everything is part of me, I am still in command of my own self, being able to touch, feel, think, act and interact. But as I express my desires, dreams, ambitions, ideals, or even grievances, I cannot but find myself touching and being touched by the presence of others that are part of me and together, we make up everything to become what I call 'me'.

It is in the spirit of togetherness as well as belongingness that one gets to realize one's own self. Without this spirit, the person may just linger and stay with himself, not realizing that by opening up to others, he is opening up to himself, enriching and enlarging his soul for his own good and benefit.

We need others, and others need us too. We need one another not only for the purpose of getting the pieces of Nature together and make them into things that we could live by, such as the food that we eat and the place that we live. We need one another for affection, for friendship, for trust, for security, for strength, for unity, and for identity.

Through bonded in a group, we get to understand how we

are just one piece out of the many pieces of a jigsaw puzzle that when each and every one of us are put together, we get a picture of how we all appear collectively, and from this collective appearance, we get to know how each and every one of us looks like individually.

This way, in benefitting himself, one benefits others and, in benefitting others, benefits himself. He is one who, in enjoying life, others get to enjoy it too. He feels glad and his spirit elevated when others are happy, and he feels sad and sombre when others are suffering. He is, like what Prophet Muhammad said, that 'None of you can consider himself faithful to his religion until he loves for his fellow brethren what he loves for himself.' Such a person is a person whose self opens to other selves. He is the gate through which love and compassion, sharing and caring, sympathy and empathy, flow through and light the hearts of others.

◆

The basis of human togetherness is *taqwa* or putting God as one's priority in life and it is this priority that becomes the measurement of one's humanity. We humans tend to compare ourselves with others through such aspects like wealth, birthright, skin colour, and race and use these aspects to grade ourselves as being higher or lower in terms of being human.

But the Qur'an says, 'O mankind. We have created you from a single male and female and made you into peoples and tribes so that you may know one another. The most noble among you in the sight of God are those most God-conscious (*atqa-kum*) amongst you (Q49:13).'

When God is made the basis of one's relationship with other humans, there is no room to look down upon others. One may be rich but if his wealth is acquired through ill-gotten means such as through cheating or corruption, then in the sight of God, his wealth is worth its place in hell. And, if a person whose wealth is only to satisfy his own pleasures and also to show off to others, being rich makes the person a poor soul in the sight of God.

Therefore, being in togetherness with our fellow humans in the spirit of *taqwa* is the basis of our identity as a human being.

◆

But togetherness is not only with our fellow human beings. We have around us the world of Nature with the air that we breathe, the birds and beasts that roam the skies, the water on earth that we drink with delight, the creatures of the streams and oceans that add to life's sunshine, and the green grasses and meadows that cool our sights. The wonderful world of Nature makes our life delightful because it is the source and resource for our biological needs. It is also the source and resource for our artistic imagination and expression. But most of all, it is the source and resource for our thoughts, beliefs, and actions.

The world of Nature is a little door that opens to another dimension of existence, namely, the world of the invisible and the origin of our being. In this sense, the world of Nature is *ayat,* or signs, that allude to the higher meaning of things. The world of Nature enlightens our intelligence, arouses our passion for knowing, ignites our curiosity, and challenges our determination to transform the world into a paradise for living. And in the course of all these, we are brought back, through our enlightened intelligence, to a source that is the cause of all that is, which is none other than God, none other than *Allah*.

Needless to say, a life of togetherness is a life bonded into all that is part of our existence without which we would never be able to realize a holistic and wholesome personality through which we enjoy life in our individual and personal capacity.

13

Life with Nature

*W*hen we look at the world around us, whether we call it Nature, environment, ecology, or surrounding, we find its inhabitants—be they the birds that roam the skies, the hills and forests that stand firm on the ground, the grasses and meadows with their lush green pastures, the animals that roam in the wilderness, or the rivers and streams that flow gently in their winding paths—astounding us with the beauty of their existence. These things are for us to benefit, and we benefit from them as things we consume for our biological sustenance and life's continuance.

But as human beings, it is in our nature to see these things not solely as items of consumption. We look at these things and we are amazed at their patterns of behaviour that are harmonious and orderly. The Greeks call this harmonious and orderly existence Cosmos, or orderly fashion, as against Chaos, or disorderly fashion.

For some people, the rhythms of Nature are a symphony of Maths such that Nature is their source of inspiration for mathematical orderliness, and they see in Nature the geometrical proportions of its designs that with these geometrical proportions, they could carve out living places that are in harmony with their surroundings.

In some religious traditions, the world of Nature is imagined as a relationship between the sun and its rays, or the centre and its periphery, so that whatever is at the periphery is the offshoot of the centre.

Christians, for instance, imagine Jerusalem as the centre of the universe, and all other places were designed pointing in the direction of Jerusalem.

The Forbidden City in China at one time became the prototype model of all living quarters in Beijing or Peking and beyond, as the Forbidden City is the symbol of the meeting place between heaven and human. This is the dwelling place of the emperor, whom the Chinese call *Tian Tzu*, or Son of Heaven. Ironically, even the mosques in China were all designed according to this pattern, basically a square or a rectangular shape, and the Chinese call the square '*fang*'. In fact, the Ka'bah, Makkah, and Islam were all called '*Tian Fang*', or heavenly square. Even today, the most important place in a city where people gather is called a Square.

For some people, Nature is a symphony of orchestra, where Nature provides the inspiration, as well as the locus, for the art of sound. Muslims, for instance, have the *azan,* or the call to prayer, where Nature provides the space, time, and moment for the sound to emerge from the silence of dawn and to descend into the silence of the night. Through the *azan*, life springs into action, and through the *azan*, life descends into quietude. Thus, the *azan* is the meeting point between sound and silence, activity and stillness, life and lifelessness, waking and sleeping, light and darkness, manifest and hidden. The *azan*, in other words, brings the Muslim to his meeting point between God and man, his beginning and his end, his life and his lifelessness, his activity and his stillness.

For some people, Nature is a symphony of living things coming and working together to ensure the continuity of existence. Nature is seen as a living organism where labour and pain were poured into life by its inhabitants. From the rain and earth, to the plants and animals, and to the human inhabitants, all of them contribute their part to ensure life could go on. Human beings exhale carbon dioxide so that plants could live, and in turn, plants exhale oxygen so that humans could live. So Nature, in this sense, is the unity of life where everything in it co-operates with each other to make life happens.

For some people, Nature is a hidden secret of methods to be extracted by the human mind in order to understand Nature's workings, and these methods could equally be applied into the observation, study, and prediction of things to happen, including human events. Today, we call it 'science'. The word 'science' is derived from the Latin '*scientia*', meaning 'knowledge'. But in today's discourse, science refers to the knowledge of something, or some event, that was previously unknown to us but could be known through the use of the scientific method of investigation. A simple example would be the weather forecast. Through the use of the scientific method, meteorologists could track the movement of the clouds and climatic change, and inform us in advance about the weather condition for the coming days.

◆

Therefore, Nature is a beautiful object of existence that acts as a veil between us and the reality that lies behind its appearance. The veil is, of course, the many objects of Nature—such as the skies and the rains, the plants and the animals, and even human beings themselves.

Through our human intellect, we could 'lift' this veil and see the reality behind it. We could 'lift' the veil because these objects of Nature contain meanings, messages, and purposes that our human intellect could discern. These meanings, messages, and purposes appear to us in many guises—as a mathematical model, as an organismic creature, as a symphony of orchestra, as a machine-like thing such as a watch, as a body of method, or as a romantic piece of poetry. Through these many guises, our mind not only becomes curious, but also fascinated, by them.

Because Nature stands between us and the reality that lies behind it, any form of representation of this reality through an object of Nature (such as a stone, wood, or human) only blocks this reality from reaching our human intellect. We are therefore unable to make out what this reality is precisely.

The acknowledgement of this reality, that Muslims call *Allah*, is part of our human nature, irrespective of how others would call it. Islam does not refute the acknowledgement of God by any other name, whether it is *Tuhan* in Malay or *Tian* in Chinese, but what it does is to place this acknowledgement in its proper perspective, so that God is recognized rightfully with regard to who He is, and also with regard to what He means for our existence through the many splendours and mysteries of Nature that He embellishes, for us to wonder and be captivated by their beauty.

Things of Nature are like the glittering stars, becoming reflections of the source that supplies their presence, which is God. They are called *ayat* or signs because they contain the meanings, messages, and wisdoms of what humanity constitutes. The *ayat* also act as a bridge that leads the human intellect back to God.

When our human intellect is properly connected to God, we will see the things around us in proper perspective, regard them in the proper way, and behave towards them in the proper manner. Such is the magnanimity of Nature in human life.

Needless to say, all of Nature speaks of God and all of Nature leads the human mind and intelligence back to God.

14

A Life of Thought

A life of Islam is a life of God or Godly life. This seems to give the impression that such a life is everything about God and little about us humans, that we humans are a weak and passive lot, and since we are always occupied with the thought of God, we tend to neglect the world we live in when we should be occupied with the many challenges that we humans are facing.

To be thoughtful is to ponder and reflect. Islam is a religion that exhorts its adherents to be thoughtful and to ponder and reflect upon the life they are having.

The Qur'an is replete with verses that exhort us to think, ponder, reflect, and contemplate. 'Certainly in the creation of the heavens and the earth, and the succession of night and day, are signs for those who digest their significance (Q3:190)'. And, 'Do they not look at the camels, how they are made? And at the sky, how it is raised high? And at the mountains, how

they are fixed firm? And at the earth, how it is spread out?
(Q88:17-21)'.

◆

The world that spreads before our eyes is a collection of *ayat* or
signs. 'We will show them Our signs in the universe, and in
their own selves, until it becomes manifest to them that this
(the Quran) is the truth (41:53)'.

Through the *ayat* or signs we are brought to something
farther and further than what appears before our eyes which
will explain our life's mission on earth.

Water is a sign that we come across every moment of our
life. When we hold a cup of water, we ought to realize that the
water connects us to every other thing that has to do with life.

As humans, we are endowed with a rich imagination and
creativity of the mind, so that the water we drink comes in all
kinds of varieties. We drink coffee, but coffee that comes in all
kinds of fancy names. We drink americano, cappuccino, café
latte, and café au lait.

Some of us drink cappuccino because it is tasty. Some of
us drink cappuccino because it gives us a sense of our
identity—modern and up-to-date. Some of us drink
cappuccino because it warms the body. Thus, drinking
cappuccino, and drinking all kinds of coffee that come with all
kinds of names, for that matter, means different things to
different people.

No matter what drinking coffee means to a person, for a
Muslim, when he sips a cup of coffee, he remembers that the
coffee he drinks is only possible because of the water that

makes it possible, and the water is possible because there is a giver of water, and this giver of water is one who attends to the needs of mankind all the time. This giver of water so that life is made possible and the varieties of drinks can be made available, is thus the ALL-Caring, the ALL-Giving, the ALL-Loving, the ALL-Seeing, the ALL-Knowing, the ALL-Hearing and the ALL of everything. He is *Allah*, the source of human life, the source of human enjoyment, the source of human happiness.

◆

Because *Allah* brings us into existence, He takes upon Himself to provide for us, take care of us, and make sure we will not do the things that will bring harm and hurt to us and to our loved ones. He tells us what we should and should not do, not because He wants to make life hard for us but because He wants to make sure we are doing the things that will bring happiness to ourselves and others.

Therefore, when a Muslim sips his cup of coffee, he remembers *Allah* who is the source of his life, remembers *Allah* who gives him the water, remembers *Allah* who gives him a creative mind that with it, he is able to make drinks of all varieties from the one same water. The Muslim also remembers that there are drinks that are harmful to the body, and there are drinks that are beneficial to it. The Muslim drinks only those that are beneficial to the body, and shuns those that bring harm to it.

Needless to say, the water we drink is indeed a story to think about health and life, and what choices we make with regard to what we take, and how with *Allah* present in our life, our choices are directed at those that will bring only good and praiseworthy consequences to our body, mind, and behaviour.

'Say: Is it the same between those who know and do not know? Surely, those who possess the depth of insight are those who constantly reflect (Q39:9)'.

That is why, for a Muslim, thinking is an integral aspect of his growth into a becoming a human being of the noblest kind because in thinking, he connects with the signs that are spread before his eyes and relates them to the ultimate aims of living that will give him the big picture of his tiny presence in the universe.

15

A Life of Inquiry

*B*eing thoughtful and reflecting over the vast spectrum of creation is an aspect of living Islam. Being curious and to inquire into the vast spectrum of creation is another aspect of living Islam. Islam, after all, is a religion of the intellect and not of blind submission to God.

To recognize that there is a power, or there is sacredness, behind everything that we see around us, is part of our human nature. Some of us call it religion, some call it superstition, some call it magic, some call it totemism, and some have no names to call it. Even in modern times like ours, where religion is said to be fading into the rear of human life, traces of religiosity could still be seen in the way we regard things. 'Life is sacred' is one phrase we often come across.

The fact that we humans possess the tendency to see the presence of a power, or the presence of sacredness, behind everything that we see, touch, or feel, is an indication that it is part of our human nature to see farther into the things than what they appear before our eyes.

We want to go beyond and behind the many things that we see and look for the answers as to why these things exist. What are they really, and what are they for, actually? In some societies, the things of Nature, such as the mountains, rivers, forests and animals, are not merely things that provide biological sustenance for human living, becoming food to be consumed so that life could continue. For these societies, the world around them is a world inhabited by living forces that they believe exist but could not make out exactly what these forces are. These forces are often regarded in a negative way, in the sense that they are thought to cause harm and bring calamity to the lives of these people. In some societies, these forces appear as human superpowers, such as those found in the Greek, Roman and Hindu gods. Quite surprisingly, even in modern times, such similarity does exist, although these human superpowers appear as comic superheroes in the likes of *Superman*, *Batman*, and *Spiderman*. In some societies, such as the Chinese society, these human superpowers appear more human than god, and their presence is to regulate moral uprightness among the living.

◆

The desire to go beyond or behind the things we come across so that we could know what these things *really* are and what they mean for our existence, means that as we stretch our curiosity farther and deeper to arrive at the essences of things, we are indirectly leading ourselves to the origin and beginning of all things that exist, including our very own existence.

Again, this path leading our curiosity to the origin and beginning of everything that exists is not something alien to our human nature. When adopted children, given away when they were little babies, grew up to find that somehow they did not possess their adopted parents' look, would be curious to know who their real parents are. In other words, they want to know who they properly are, and this can only be found in the origin and beginning of their birth, the first moment of their existence on earth.

In the same way, we are not contented to stop at our parents, or grandparents, or great grandparents, and say that we are satisfied with the answer concerning our existence. Rather, we want to go farther and deeper, and ask, not only with regard to our own existence, but with regard to the existence of the human race in general, and beyond that, with regard to existence of everything there is. We want to know what the origin, the beginning, of everything, is. By knowing the origin, and beginning, of everything that exists, we could also know who we properly are as an existence called human being.

When we try to connect with the origin and beginning of things, we go beyond what we see into what we *do not* see. We may be surprised to find that the more we do not see a thing, the more our intelligence becomes enlightened because, in order to know what we do not know, our curiosity is increased and our mind would venture into territories of the unknown to find out what the unknown are.

But no matter how intelligent we may be, our mind has its

limits so that while we may arrive at the point of saying that there is a source to everything that exists, we are unable to make out precisely what this source is. When we see how objects of Nature, such as trees, stones, and even human figures, take on divine forms and become deities and gods, this only tells us the shortcomings of our human ability to make sense of the ultimate that is the source of whatever that exists and, as a result, compromised for something less but still a viable satisfaction to our curiosity.

This only means that if there was any answer at all, this answer must come from a source beyond the human mind. For that to happen, it takes the human conviction, rather than the human intelligence, to acknowledge that such possibility does exist. But how can the human intelligence become convinced that this source is the right source to believe? One way to know this is to see the range of beliefs, acts, and activities that are connected with this source.

Truth is not only about the mind proving and disproving things through logical arguments. Truth can be discerned through the range of things associated with the source that becomes the focus of belief, in terms of their consequences and meaning to human life. For instance, when one looks at how Islam spread from a centre in the barren desert of Arabia but thereafter sprouting here and there in lands from one end of the earth to another end of the earth and blossoming into a civilization with all the splendours of living, from science to arts to medicine to philosophy to law to architecture, this is self-evident of what truth is about, that beliefs, acts, and activities work in consonance to produce humans of the desirable kind who will make this world a paradise on earth and that is exactly what Islam aspires to do through an understanding of God where truth works in real life experience and not merely as a logical proposition in the mind.

Islam is a religion of inquiry that seeks to bring the mind into active participation in the purpose of creation so that the truth of heaven is brought out into the vast spectrum of creation on earth and embodied in life and living which will enable us to see how truth looks and not merely what truth is.

To inquire is an essential aspect of living Islam and the mind acts as the bridge connecting heaven and earth by connecting with the signs that spread across the horizons, turning these signs and the messages, wisdoms, and purposes couched in them into knowledge of all varieties and then use them to turn this world into a paradise for living.

Such is the place of inquiry in the life of Islam.

16

A Life of Learning

*L*earning means different things to different people. For some, learning is about seeking truth. For such persons, learning is about going behind the things we see or the things we do and seek out their principles and causes, namely, the reasons why things are what they are. In this regard, religion, for some, is the best avenue to look for the answers to the most fundamental questions about reality and truth. For some others, it is philosophy, the use of human reasoning, to arrive at the answer concerning existence. Yet, for some others, modern science is the surest way to know things, as it deals with what we can see, touch, and feel, and avoid all the wild speculations of the mind that philosophy could bring us into, as well as avoiding answers coming from religion as religion only dictates the answers without giving much room for the human mind to explore the secrets hidden in the far-end corners of the universe.

Learning, for some societies, has everything to do with the life and death of a community's identity. In the European society of medieval times where Christianity was the order of the day, theology or learning about God is the queen of knowledge, and to be a theologian is to be a highly regarded person in society because, like the warrior in medieval times, without the theologian, the European society could be thrown into disarray.

Learning is also directed at the amelioration of the human life. In this sense, learning is intended for practical purposes. Learning is to help improve the quality and quantity of the food we eat and the water we drink. Learning is to help fend off diseases by discovering the causes of the diseases and how we may combat them. Learning is to help bring out inventions so that with them, we could produce things that may enrich our life. The electricity, for instance, helps us to see at night more vividly with the fluorescent lamps compared to the oil lamps and makes the refrigerator a wonderful place to store meat, fish, and vegetable. Learning, in this regard, is not to produce theoreticians but utilitarians, namely, down-to-earth people who can put knowledge into producing material goods for the betterment of the human life. Learning is for useful purposes, not about things for admiration and awe. Learning is about producing *useful* human beings, people with useful or utilitarian value.

Learning was, for many societies in the past, about producing *good* human beings even as it produces *useful* human beings. Homes were the first and most basic place of education. Parents teach their children through practical

conduct of behaviour, with themselves being the role model.
Schools were next in importance, and parents sent their
children to school to be moulded into upright persons.
Teachers, in this regard, occupy a very noble position in
society, and were highly regarded for their moral inasmuch as
for their knowledge. In the Chinese society of ancient times,
men of learning occupied the top of the social strata (these
would be, not only teachers, but magistrates, court officials,
and ministers as well. Holding public offices is not only a pride
to one's self, but to one's parents and children, kith and kin,
neighbours and friends as well), followed by those who tilled
the lands i.e. agrarians, those who worked in the production
industry i.e. artisans, and those who were engaged in business
and trade, in that sequence. Those who carved their careers
from profit-making activities occupied the lowest rank in the
social order. Put simply, for one to become a lawyer in today's
world means nothing to the traditional Chinese view of society
if becoming a lawyer means first and foremost, making the
legal profession a profit-making venture, and putting law and
order as a secondary importance. Becoming a lawyer would
only be looked up as a respectful profession if the knowledge
and practice of law are reflected in the lawyer's personality, and
not as a means for material gains.

Coming to today's society, learning, for many of us, is
about having a good career, a secure job, and a fat income. It is
about how much money we can earn and what kinds of things
we can splash the money on. It is about the kind of knowledge
that could make us wealthy and to afford a life of comfort.
Learning is to make us forget all the sorrows of life and instead,
seek a life of enjoyment. Learning is no longer about seeking

what is real and true, nor is it about seeking what is good and virtuous. It is about making money. There was a story about this young boy who went around from place to place to sell video CDs. One day his mother called him and asked him to focus on his studies instead. 'Mom,' he said. 'Why should I be going to school and studying so hard?' 'Well, my son,' said his mother. 'So that you will be able to enter university, get a good job after that, earn a good income, and lead a comfortable life.' The boy looked at his mother, frowned, and said, 'Mom, isn't this what I am doing? Earning a good income and leading a comfortable life? And the best part is, I don't have to go to university to make good money.'

◆

Al-Ghazali, a celebrated scholar of Islam who lived in the 11th century, said that in whatever we seek in life, we should not lose sight of two sets of knowledge that will govern our pursuits of life, irrespective of whether these pursuits are intended to satisfy our queries (asking questions, such as about our purpose of life), for practical purposes (putting knowledge to good use, such as finding cures for diseases), or to produce things for the fulfillment of our needs (for instance, inventions that improve our living condition, such as cars and televisions).

We must relate our pursuits of life to the first set of knowledge and which is (1) knowledge of self (2) knowledge of God (3) knowledge of this world, and (4) knowledge of the next world.

Thereafter, the knowledge of these four, in turn, must be

related to the knowledge of another four which constitute the second set of knowledge and these are (1) *ibadat* or things that keep us in touch with God (2) *adat* or things that keep us in touch with life that are necessary for everyday living (3) *muhlikat* or things that are destructive to our well-being in the form of eroding vices (4) *munjiyat* or things that contribute to our well-being in the form of redeeming virtues.

Fulfilling our dreams and wishes is something we always look forward to, and often with excitement too. Young children are always excited about the prospect of growing up and becoming adults fast, and dream of becoming a doctor, or an engineer, or a lawyer, and all those professions that will give them the feel-good image about their self-pride and identity. Learning, for these young aspirants, is about looking to the future with big ambitions and big achievements. The world, for these budding young people, is a temptation for endless pursuits of life.

But one Western philosopher puts it rather succinctly that even as we lead our life forward we also tend to think it backward. It happens that, for many of us, at some point in time, we would look back at life and ask where our goals are taking us. We would be asking if there is anything more, anything beyond, and anything further than just going after the material satisfaction of life. We will query upon such questions like, 'Who am I,' 'Where do I come from,' 'What am I doing in this world,' and 'Where do I go after I die.' These questions, incidentally, are intimately connected to the knowledge of self, God, this world, and the next world.

As such, our existence is a continuous and an unbreakable connection with God so that the *ibadat* such as the five times daily prayer, serve as the spokes connecting us and God and sustaining this unbreakable connection throughout our life. The *ibadat* are an essential aspect of our existence because through them, our life's activities or *adat*, are rendered truthful, meaningful, purposeful, useful, and joyful, and we get a clear picture about how we go about with life.

As we pursue the many needs for the fulfillment as well as for the continuity and progress of the earthly life, we are guided by our *ibadat* that keep us in check about what things that can wreak our well-being, destroy our humanity, render our life pointless, and making our existence meaningless. These are the *muhlikat*, destructive-causing elements. *Ibadat*, in this regard and on their part, keep us in check from sliding into the *muhlikat*, or if we ever fall into the pit of errors and committing the vices, our *ibadat* will help return us to our original good self and this is achieved through the *munjiyat*, the redeeming virtues (such as regret, dislike for vices, love for rightness and goodness).

Thus, with these two sets of knowledge, our journey of learning can deliver us to become the very purpose of our existence, which is to become a *khalifah* who is grounded in learning as the basis of his human becoming but a learning that brings into union heaven and earth in the person of the human.

17

A Life of Work

*W*hy do we work? What do we achieve with work and what do we gain by working?

For many living in today's society, work is survival of livelihood. Debts are more than earnings, as prices of things have soared beyond what one could imagine. Basic necessities of life have become more and more difficult to obtain unless one has the money to afford them. Food has become rather expensive, and if one is someone who is in the habit of eating out, this could drain the purse or pocket. Education has also become expensive because education is no longer about being a good human being, but about how much money one can make. Health is also another area of concern as hospital bills are skyrocketing and if one does not have insurance, how could one pay for these bills? In today's world that is characterized by the computer craze, new and more sophisticated products are churned out every now and then and the young ones especially, do not want to miss out on these. Where is the money coming from to afford these gadgets? So parents have to work, students have to work, and even the little ones have to start looking for jobs, or otherwise one will slip into poverty and cannot even afford what beggars could. Thus, to work is to be able to eat, sleep, and find a place for shelter.

For some, work is self-pride, that something giving us the drive, enthusiasm, and spirit to show others what we are made of. Getting straight A's, or getting four flat on the CGPA, or getting into Cambridge, Oxford, or Harvard is self-pride, not only for one's self, but also for one's parents and family members. It speaks a lot about the workload, focus, and hard work put into the efforts to achieve such results. It also speaks a lot about the parents' role in their children's success story. Thus, self-pride is to be able to compete with others and come out on top of them. For some, self-pride is to practise a high level of virtue and morality, so that one is recognized as an upright person in society, and be trusted in any business dealings. And, for some, self-pride is to hold public office, such as becoming a magistrate, or a policeman, or a teacher, because public servants put the interest of others before self, and sacrifice their time and energy for the well-being of others.

For some, work itself is religion. Hindus, for instance, see work as the outcome of one's previous life. It is the karma of work that determines what one's next life would be, for better or for worse. If the good karma overweighs the bad karma, one who is a bellboy could well be on his way to becoming a priest, the highest and most noble human dignity in the Hindu view of life. For Christians of the Protestant faith, work is the measurement of whether one is elected into heaven. Good works do not guarantee salvation as it is faith alone that guarantees it, but good works are indications that the faith one professes is an acceptable one, and thereby salvation is assured.

To summarize, work is that by which we get to realize our desires, wants, and even dreams. These are needs that we seek to fulfill without which life falls short of expectations and meaningfulness. We have basic needs to fulfill, such as food, clothing, shelter, and healthcare. These are *biological* needs. As human beings, we are not contented with having only shelter. We want to make the shelter a home that has nice designs and decorations, and looks colourful too. In short, as humans, we crave for things pleasant, lovely, and beautiful. These are *aesthetical* needs. We also need warmth, love, and affection. The fulfillment of needs may be less meaningful if we do not achieve them together, or even share what we have with others, for caring is a very precious aspect of humanity. But above all, we have feelings for one another because 'I am what I am because of who we all are.' These are *affective* needs. We need to feel safe and protected from harm and danger, to our life, property, and mind. These are *safety* needs. We need values for our life, about what is right and wrong, good or bad, so that decisions that we make will have positive consequences as well as avoid putting ourselves and others in harm's way. These are *axiological* needs. As human beings, we seek not only what is basic and sufficient, but we aspire to bring the basic to the level of sophistication, so that we comprehend and understand things at the highest and deepest level possible that would reveal to us their true and real nature. These are *intellectual* needs. We also desire for *self-expression* or *cultural* needs, needs by which we display our preference for how things look, including about the way we appear as a person. Being humans, we have ambitions, we desire to be motivated, we want to achieve things, and we wish to turn dreams into realities. We are not contented with only having to eat, having a place to stay, or having clothes to wear. We look at the world around us, and we want to transform the world into much more than what we could imagine. These needs, the drives to turn something into something more, are *self-esteem* needs. Through the self-esteem needs, we want to end up as somebody with an identity, to be able to tell others this is what I am. This is *self-realization* need. Finally, there are the *spiritual* needs. For many of us, life is unfulfilled and incomplete if it is not a blessed life, a life that gives us not only a sense of satisfaction, but a sense of serenity and peace. With a life that is blessed, we can go about fulfilling all our other needs, knowing that we have been truthful, righteous, virtuous, and conscientious in our quest to fulfil our needs. All the needs as mentioned are necessary for us to be an all-round human being. They are all related to one another without which, our human identity will not take shape. Work, through the fulfillment of needs, defines our human identity, about who we are, about who I am.

In the same way, work defines the meaning of a Muslim. It is through work that a Muslim is able to see what kind of person he is, and ultimately, what human identity he is carrying.

◆

In Islam, work is called *amal*. *Amal* may refer to individual acts, or activities, or livelihood.

The Qur'an mentions *amal salih* or works that are righteous, virtuous, good, and praiseworthy, all the time. All of us humans are required to do not just *amal* but *amal salih*. Why is the emphasis on works that are *salih*?

In the first place, for a Muslim, work carried out must be predicated, or based, or grounded in God. God is the point of reference for work. God is the point of departure for work. God is the point of return for work. What does this mean?

When a Muslim works, he is governed by a set of guidelines about how he fulfills his needs. These guidelines are intended to protect, preserve, and promote the well-being of the essential aspects of his humanity, so that he will become, as well as function, as a wise, true, good, virtuous, kind, loving, pleasurable and beautiful human being. These guidelines are collectively known as the *Shariah*. The guidelines' purposes, namely, the protection, preservation, and promotion of the essential aspects of humanity, are known as *maqasid al-shariah* or *objectives of shariah*. The well-being i.e. essential aspects of humanity that the *shariah* seeks to protect, preserve, and promote are known as *maslaha* or *masalih*, and these are the well-being of religion (*din*), self and life (*nafs*), mind ('*aql*), kith and kin (*nasl*), property (*mal*) and dignity ('*ird*).

Religion (*din*) is the constitution, blueprint, and guideline of a person's life, purpose, and destiny. It is the reference point for the answers that one seeks pertaining to his human identity. Through religion, one knows his origin, life, and purpose in this world. Through religion, one knows how one relates to all that exists, from God to everything in the Unseen world, to everything that we could see in this world. Religion puts us in proper perspective of our beliefs, thoughts, actions and interactions.

The self (*nafs*) is our body and the vitality of life that comes with it. It connects us to everything around us, from humans to animals to plants. The body is a fragile entity that could succumb to harm and injury, and great care has to be taken of it. The body, apart from being a biological and physical entity, is also the locus of our personal worthiness so that nothing can wrest the rights that come with it, such as taking the life of a person without just cause or slandering the physical appearance of a person. The body is the region of our self-respect, and we must do the necessary to make our body a respectable part of us.

Besides us, we have our parents and children, kith and kin, all related through a common bloodline (*nasl*). These are our flesh and blood, as well as our laughter and tears, pain and joy. Thus, taking care of our body also means to take care of our loved ones, because we and our loved ones are, biologically and psychologically, related. We are the body extension of our parents, and our children, our progeny, are the body extension of us. Therefore all care must be taken in relation to how we are related to our kith and kin in terms of flesh and blood, and how we behave towards one another in this relationship. Thus, intermingling between opposite sexes must be such that both sides must know what they should and should not do that will not result in undesirable consequences to the body, which will then have psychological and social implications upon the person. Religion spells out the wisdoms for the respect of the body, and carves out boundaries for the relationship, and promises the joys one gets if the rules of relationship are followed, or conversely, the agonies and pains if the rules are broken.

Property or wealth (*mal*), in its broadest sense, refers to whatever that contributes to the material fulfillment of life. Property or wealth could be tangible things, such as land, cattle, and homes, or intangible ones such as knowledge, technology, services, or even money. In our acquisition of wealth, as well as the use of it, we are confronted with the question about how we acquire it, whether rightly or wrongly, and whether the wealth we acquire is beneficial or harmful to our well-being. And, whether we share a portion of our wealth with others, especially the underprivileged. There are those of us who are wealthy but not thrifty and spend our wealth unnecessarily. There are those of us who are wealthy but nevertheless stingy so that we find it hard to even share a little of our wealth with those in need. But there are those of us who are wealthy but see joy in sharing our wealth with others, and are generous with our contribution to the well-being of others. Thus, we are of diverse personalities when it comes to how we treat property and wealth. In order that we get the best from the property and wealth we possess, there are rules about how we acquire them, use them, and share them with others. With these rules, we will be guided and moulded into a personality that cares, and shares.

Besides a body, we have a mind. Our mind (*'aql*) is our resource for thought, imagination, and creativity. With the mind, we explore the rich resources of our world and turn them into a wonderful place to live in. With the mind, we imagine turning the world into some kind of Foreverland that we hope would be our paradise on earth. With the mind, we become creative about what we eat and drink, what we wear and display, and what we use and benefit. But most importantly, with the mind, we seek answers to the most fundamental questions about our human existence - where we came from, what we are doing in this world, what is the best life, and where we are heading in our afterlife. To be enlightened about these questions is to be enlightened about why, in some of our actions, there are commands to do them, the prohibitions to avoid them, and the choices to do or not to do them. Through the mind and the answers we get from these fundamental questions of life, we will be able to know why there are boundaries to the way we deal with our identity, body, progeny, property, mentality, and activity.

Dignity (*'ird*) is our personal pride. It is an integral part of our existence, like water is to life or soul is to body, where in the event any harm is done to it, the person suffers both emotionally and mentally and for some of us, the loss of the desire to go on living. The tongue, in this regard, is a very deadly place to destroy one's dignity. It is through slander, backbiting, lies, and deceit, to name some of the vices of the tongue, that one's dignity can be destroyed. Backbiting is likened to eating the flesh of one's fellow human because in saying things behind one's back especially if the things said are those that degrade his integrity and personality, it can cause others who hear them to form a negative perception of the person and shun him altogether. Therefore, dignity is high on the list deserving protection as it is an essential aspect of humanity that if any harm is caused to it, it can cause one to lose his desire to go on living because his personal pride has been snatched away from him.

Work should make us realize that in fulfilling our needs, there are guidelines to be observed, objectives to be achieved, and a personality to be shaped, such that our life becomes satisfied yet meaningful as the work we do delivers us to the realization of what it is to be human, and, ultimately, the wisdom of being God's vicegerent on earth, one who is wise and truthful, righteous and good, loving and caring, humble and beautiful.

18

A Life of Guidance

For Muslims, to know *Allah*, it is He who tells us who He is, not we ourselves who make out His identity, that He is such and such. *Allah* communicates to us about how He could be known and understood, and this He does through His words (called *wahy* or revelation) which are delivered through a group of human beings known as prophets or messengers (called *nabi* and *rasul*).

Islam teaches that the first human beings were Adam and Hawa (or Eve) and Adam was the first prophet and messenger. There are thousands of prophets and messengers from the time of Adam until the last prophet and messenger, who is Prophet Muhammad. The message of Islam began with Adam and ended with Muhammad and it passed through some of the most important personalities known in human history, such as Ibrahim or Abraham, Musa or Moses, Dawud or David, and Isa or Jesus. But it is with Muhammad that the message of

Islam and the revelation from heaven culminated and ended. From the time of Muhammad onward, anyone following the path of Islam follows only the path of Muhammad.

Prophet Muhammad was given a collection of revelation known as Al-Qur'an. The Qur'an, the very word of *Allah*, along with the actions and teachings of Prophet Muhammad known as the Sunnah, become the two main sources of the Muslim life about how they think about life and how they go about with life.

◆

Prophet Muhammad said, 'I leave you two things that if you hold on to them firmly, you will not misstep in your actions. These are the Qur'an and my Sunnah.'

With the Qur'an and the Sunnah, every Muslim now has two sources to guide them in their life. To put the teachings of the Qur'an and the Sunnah into action, we need a third element and it is the intellect or *'aql*.

As human beings, we are not passive recipients of knowledge and instruction, acting and behaving like some kind of robot without question. Rather, we are of such nature that it requires our active participation and engagement with the knowledge and instruction we receive where we are to interpret and relate them to the environment we live in so that we could make sense of what we are doing. Also, we are creatures with creativity, always feeling excited at the chance to demonstrate our ability to produce new ideas, new things, and new environments from the existing knowledge and instruction we have, and not merely feeling contented with following them outright without even inquiring about what they are and what they do to us.

The Qur'an and the Sunnah are not static words that merely direct us about how we go about with life. On the contrary, they contain oceans of possible meanings that require the use of the intellect to fathom, understand, and digest the spirit behind the words so that we could synchronize and align the intents and purposes of the Qur'an and the Sunnah with the realities and situations of our human condition that differ from place to place and culture to culture. The Qur'an and the Sunnah, namely, divine revelation and prophetic mission, in this regard, serve as the text for our life's story while the world that we live in serves as its context, and the role of the intellect is to find a meeting point between the two about how we think and live our life.

◆

When Prophet Muhammad appointed Muaz bin Jabal as governor of Yemen, he asked Muaz how he would decide when a case is brought before him and to which Muaz said, 'I shall look into the Qur'an.' Then the Prophet asked him that if he did not find anything in the Qur'an what would he do and to which Muaz said, 'I will then look into the Sunnah of the Prophet.' The Prophet then asked Muaz that should he not find anything in his Sunnah, how would he proceed with the case and to which Muaz said, 'I will exercise my own judgment but will not deviate from the Qur'an and the Sunnah.'

Thus, participation on our part is inevitable if we are to put the words of heaven into action and to make them alive and relevant to what we do in our everyday situation and condition.

The intellect is a very important and significant aspect of our humanity but it has its limitations and constraints such as, for instance, about making the necessary decisions regarding our actions. This is further compounded by the fact that our humanity is also constituted by passions and desires, those urges inciting us to satisfy our needs and wants but having little regard about whether they are good or bad, right or wrong, in the fulfillment of our unbounded desires.

The intellect could cave in to our insatiable demands to want this and that and in the event this happens, illogical and unjust consequences may follow and this would have defeated the very purpose of the intellect which is to make the kind of decisions and judgments which are right and relevant concerning our decisions and actions.

With the Qur'an and the Sunnah, divine revelation and prophetic mission, our intellect will be able to tie and ground our passions and desires in the proper perspectives of their aims and objectives so that we would have a life of bless and bliss. In addition, it would also be able to give views and make decisions that will not run contrary to the very purpose of our presence in this world.

The intellect is man's precious gift from heaven but it would become more precious if it can act firmly and consistently in ways that would bring about praiseworthy consequences and for this to happen, sources greater than the human intellect are necessary to ground the intellect on firm footing. These sources are none other than divine revelation and prophetic mission, the Qur'an and the Sunnah.

◆

With the Qur'an and the Sunnah, and along with the intellect, we can have a sense of who God, who *Allah*, is. The intellect, in this regard, has a crucial role to play to bring divine revelation, prophetic mission, and creation into a meeting point where it could relate and coordinate their meanings and intents into a coherent picture about the relationship between humans and God, humans and the world they live in, and between humans themselves so that we have a clear idea about where we came from, what this world means for us, what life is about, and what happens after we die, answers that will make us have an idea that this is who *Allah* is.

We could know *Allah* through analysis, for instance, namely, to see, observe and then make connections between what we see and the message or information from the things we are seeing. The Qur'an has time and again exhorted us to use our intellect to reflect on creation which will then bring us to the creator, which is none other than *Allah*. For instance, some of us look at the world and become fascinated by its regular, orderly, and rhythmic behaviour and this is because all the parts of the world work in unison to produce a balanced and harmonious relationship that will bring about a peaceful world to live in. For such persons, *Allah* strikes them as one who loves peace and harmony and because of that, we humans have to learn how to live together with our similarities and differences and work together to produce a peaceful world and a peaceful society.

Allah could have made us all the same and we could have a peaceful world quite easily but that is not what *Allah* wanted because by being different, *Allah* wants to see how we on our part make the effort to bring about harmony among ourselves and through the effort we make, we will understand that differences are a blessing that make us understand why working together is essential to producing the kind of society desirable.

Another way to understand *Allah* is through analogy, namely, to know something through knowing something else first.

For instance, if a child asks how earth is like, we tell the child that it is like a ball. The child knows what a ball is and by using the ball as analogy, the child then knows how earth looks. In the same way, when we look at our parents, we see how their sacrifices, love, and care, as well as their firmness and disciplinarian attitude, allowed us to become human beings that they themselves would feel proud of. If we understand this, we can understand why *Allah* is kind yet is firm with us humans.

Thus, analogy plays an effective role in knowing *Allah*. Through examples from our very own existence, we can relate to *Allah* in a profound way because it is in everyday experiences that we understand things and their consequences. In this regard, Prophet Muhammad said, '*Allah* says: O Son of Adam, I fell ill and you visited Me not. He will say: O Lord, and how shall I visit You when You are the Lord of the worlds? *Allah* will say: Did you not know that My servant so-and-so had fallen ill and you visited him not? Did you not know that had you visited him you would have found him with Me?'

The Qur'an is filled with histories and stories about peoples and persons such that they become lessons for subsequent generations. The story of Musa or Moses versus the Pharaoh occupies a lengthy space in the Qur'an and the gist of the story is about haughtiness, self-pride, and egoism when one occupies a high position and forgot that a position is for one to manifest humility and not to commit atrocity. The Pharaoh was so obsessed with his self-pride that he thought nothing could touch him to the extent that he declared himself as God by saying 'I am your Lord Most High' (Q79:24) until he realized that he was a mortal being after all when in pursuing Musa, he was swallowed by the sea and he said to himself at that instance that 'I believe that there is no god except Him whom the Children of Israel believe in: I am of those who submit (to *Allah*) (Q10:90)'.

Needless to say, knowledge, position, power, and wealth are means to become better human beings, not make a person proud, big-headed, and egoistic, showing off what he has rather than using them for the sake of everyone's good. In the eyes of Islam, the measurement of a person's worthiness is *taqwa* or God-consciousness for a person who is conscious of *Allah* knows how he should go about with his life's meaning and purpose.

Still another way of getting to know God is through looking at our actions. We have all heard the phrase that if we do good then good will come to us but if we do bad then bad will come get us. This is called retribution, namely, good is rewarded by good and evil gets its proper consequence. The Qur'an and the Prophet have enjoined us to do good deeds always and keep bad deeds away. The Qur'an says, 'You are the best of peoples raised among the humankind. You command to what is praiseworthy and shun what is blameworthy. And this is because you have *Allah* in your heart (Q3:110)'.

For some people, the world appears as a piece of art. As human beings, we like to produce things and be creative about the things we produce. Not only that, we like to see the things we produce look complete and perfect so that they would appear beautiful. It's like baking a cake that not only do we want it to taste good but that it must also look good, pleasing to the eyes and whetting the appetite. Such a cake would definitely attract anyone who sees it. If we understand why we humans are so much attracted to a thing that is complete, perfect, and beautiful, we will be able to understand why God made the world complete, perfect, and beautiful because only such a world can arouse the passion of its inhabitants to see it as a place worthwhile to live in. Only then will we understand why the Prophet said that 'Certainly *Allah* is Beautiful and He loves whatever is beautiful.'

There are many ways to know God and each way is a way to know Him by pointing to an aspect of His creation that will then point to Him whether by way of analysis, analogy, lessons from past histories, rewards and punishments, to name a few.

This is how we can know God, namely, by connecting divine revelation, prophetic mission, and the spectrum of creation into a meeting point by the wisdom of our intellection.

The mind is instrumental in turning the world into a paradise on earth, but with a guiding light from heaven on high and its torchbearer on earth in the person of a prophet, that paradise on earth may well be able to reflect the scenes, scents and smells of the paradise in heaven. And that is why a

Muslim, everyday in his prayer, always says, as taught by *Allah* to say, '*Ihdina al-sirat al-mustaqim*' meaning 'Guide us on the straight path.'

A life of guidance in therefore a life most desirable for the realization of the life of Islam.

19

A Life of Solitude

*A*s human beings, we yearn for times when we could be alone, all by ourselves. True, we cannot isolate ourselves from the larger society as they are our fellow human beings, nor can we isolate ourselves from the birds, beasts, and fishes because they complete the joyfulness of the world we live in, and we surely cannot detach ourselves from the transcendent because although it is the invisible, it is still our source and resource for thought, contemplation, and imagination.

However, as human beings, each of us is unique in our own ways, and we are unique in our own ways because each of us has a spirit, soul, mind, will, and senses, that we could exercise within the limits of our freedom, and along with these, dreams of our own that we would like to build as castles for ourselves.

Thus, to take a step back from all the things so dear to our life is not to divorce ourselves from them, but it is to move back a little and look at ourselves in relation to them. What do we see in us and what do we see in them? What is different yet common between us and them? How are we and they mirror reflections of one another?

We are connected to all that is dear to us through wisdom, love, virtue, perfection, and trust. If we do not cultivate these fundamental values of the heart, nurture them, see them grow into illuminating forces of our personality, and extend them into the hearts of others, we will get the opposite of their praiseworthy values - ignorance, self-interest, vices, and betrayal, the result of which is injustice to the self and others in terms of our attitude and action.

A time by ourselves would allow us to reflect upon our needs as well as our deeds, and about whether we have become wiser, more sympathetic, more righteous, more refined, and more trustworthy in our character.

◆

When we reflect upon our needs and deeds, we get to understand why God brought us into existence. Through the fulfillment of needs, we get to enjoy life and all the pleasures that come with it. But we have to work in order to get to enjoy these needs. True, we work so that we are able to fulfill the basic necessities of life. But we also work so that we could improve the quality of life. This says a lot about who we are as human beings. We are a breed of species that stops at nothing to build a paradise on earth. Through work we get to realize our dreams and fantasies, and it is through work that we get to know the worth of our human dignity. But alone, we cannot construct a paradise on earth. It is through togetherness with others that our dreams could come true. Therefore, work brings out other important aspects of our humanity, that is to say, the aspects of sharing, caring, and loving for others - compassion, so to speak.

Compassion for our fellow humans is extended to include the inhabitants in the world of Nature because in trying to transform the dense jungles into habitable places, we should not destroy the green environment that is also the source of our life's sustenance. When we destroy the sources and resources that are our life's partners, we inevitably destroy our own life as a result. Therefore, we need to be righteous in our behaviour towards others, practise trustworthiness in our relationship with them, and learn to be wise in our thought about them.

When this is said and done, we will realize that the purpose why God brought us into this world is for us to discover those precious things in our humanity that make us unique and special and thus qualify us to be God's beloved so that even our insufficiencies are blessings towards the path of greater humanity if, and only if, we make God the centre of our existence.

◆

God is inevitably the centre of life. From birth until death, from sleeping to waking, from infant age until old age, from the time one is studying to the time one is working, in times of wellness as well as sickness, and during leisure, rest, and retirement—God is the focal point for all our activities. But why is it necessary to be in touch with God? To be in touch with God is to be in touch with everything concerning life. It is with God that we know why we are here in this world and, with it, how we are able to go about doing things with purpose and meaning. But how are we in touch with God, sense His presence, and understand His relevance to our life?

One way to see this is to think that since God is the reason for our existence, it follows that, in whatever we do, all credit goes to God, and all worship is about God, for it is God that matters most in the script of human life.

Another way of seeing it is to think that our relationship with God is one of creditor and debtor. We owe this life to God. Thus, whatever God asks us to do, we do them. Once these tasks have been carried out, we go about with life the way we want them, and God does not interfere with our life except in circumstances when we need Him.

A third way of looking at the situation is to think that in our attachment to God, we get to realize our human meaning. The more we are into God, the more we are into ourselves. God's meaningfulness to our life is such that as we attempt to understand God's presence in our life, we get to understand how this life makes all the sense with God as the focal point of our beliefs, thoughts, expressions, and actions. Among the three, the third view appears the most compatible.

How is it possible for us to know God and know what He means for our existence, more so when we cannot see Him? We cannot see God but we can arrive at Him through looking, observing, and reflecting at ourselves and what is around us.

We do this by using our intellect. Perhaps this is the secret of the invisibility of God. God lay hidden from us but that is because He wants us to know that there is a unique aspect in our human constitution called the intellect, that when it is awakened and put into good use, will reveal the world and everything in it for us to be captivated by their splendour as well as their benefit for us. With the intellect, the world we live in is transformed into a garden of delight to inhabit, and we come to know that God has brought into existence a precious gem. And that precious gem is us, and our intellect is the best gift of life that we could ever imagine to make life in this world a worthwhile venture.

◆

For many of us, the intellect is often identified with the mind that is located in the brain. It is the thinking, analyzing, and judging ability of it. This however is partially true. The intellect is not the mind alone but everything of its ability: to know, sense, and feel, whether the cognizance aspect of it, the passion aspect of it, the compassion aspect of it, the emotive aspect of it, the spiritual aspect of it, the aesthetical aspect of it, and the conscience and justice aspect of it.

Man's intellect is his connecting point between him and God. Our surrounding, in this regard, is the intermediary through which we connect with God via the many signs around us.

When we connect with the world, we find ourselves in touch with all those things that give us the pleasures of life. Despite the many shortcomings, tribulations, and challenges, it cannot be denied that we humans find life in this world a pleasurable enterprise to undertake and venture into, even treating the shortcomings, tribulations, and challenges as blessings in disguise to motivate, fortify, and spur our determination to make this world an enjoyable place to live. We work hard and work smart to turn this world into a paradise on earth, one that sometimes makes us think it is ours to own, to do whatever we want with it, and be master of the world, if not the universe.

It is this overwhelming excitement, and, for some of us, obsession, with the world and what it could offer us that would cause us humans to overlook what this world means for us essentially and ultimately, and as a consequence, get ourselves to attach to the world than attach to God. The world now becomes everything for us, even becoming the focal point of our life, and God instead is alienated to the periphery of our existence, needed and sought only in times of haplessness and hopelessness. When this happens, we become disconnected from God and assume full ownership of our own ability. Our lusts, passions, and desires override all the other aspects of our intellect so that we end up being subservient to the world than being subservient to God. As a result, we become disengaged from God, become individualistic in our pursuits of life, and end up as a selfish rather than a selfless person.

But God is a loving God. We are after all His beloved. No matter how much we become alienated from Him, there is always room to make up for our shortcomings, and, to reconnect with Him. Forgetfulness is, after all, a human trait. And to forgive is God's magnanimous gift to mankind. Feeling sorry for oneself is a human trait, and to seek forgiveness from God is a magnanimous act that would elevate the stature of our human quality.

A time of solitude is a time for us to take a step back from our attachment to the world and all the affairs of everyday living we are engaged with, and in that moment of solitude, we turn to God to reflect on our deeds and misdeeds and see how we can move forward to become a better person for the rest of the life remaining of us.

20

Life Goes On

It is a remarkable part of our human nature that while we are rooted in this world of earthly life, we also desire for a place out there that we have never seen but believe it exists, a place where life goes on and on without stopping and where everything is sweet singing and pleasant living.

For some of us, somewhere over the rainbow is a place called paradise, where life is pleasure and leisure, with no worries about whether we have a place to shelter, enough food to eat, or stay healthy from diseases. Paradise is where life sweetest and most pleasant is found and, above all, it is everlasting where we do not grow old. Who do not wish for such a life?

But what does it take for me, or us, to enter the paradise of our childhood dream?

The answer is, we have to make life in this world a paradise on earth. Making this world a paradise on earth? Isn't paradise something of the afterlife?

While it is true that paradise or heaven is an afterlife thing, it is in this worldly life that we start to construct our life of eternity so that when we travel to that world after we die, it is there waiting with its gates opened for us to enter and dwell. But how do we construct our life of eternal bliss in a world of profanity that we are living in right now?

Rivers flowing in the garden of the hereafter is a reality of the next world, yet it is connected to the river flowing in this earthly world through the reality of its use, purpose, and wisdom. The water connects the two worlds, and it invokes in a person the realization of the pleasure it gives for the body, its necessity for the human life, and most of all, it awakens in the mind and heart the question about what water is to existence as a whole. Therefore, the water we are gifted from heaven, we should use our rich imagination to produce all kinds of tasty but healthy drinks, not drinks that cause us to lose the stability of our mental state such as drunkenness, or those which are poisonous to our body, or even those that would cause health problems, such as diabetes.

Paradise or heaven is a blissful and happy experience of life. So, to have a blissful and happy life in the hereafter, we must first construct a blissful and happy life on earth. The little of the wonder and splendour we see of a paradise on earth alludes to more of such in the paradise of heaven.

That there is a life beyond the one we have on earth, and that it is more blissful and wonderful, means that all the efforts we put into making the world a paradise on earth is not a vain pursuit after all! Life is not all earth as it will continue into the realm of the hereafter. This surely must be good news for those who toil and sweat for a life in this world as it will encourage them to put in more efforts into making this earthly life an even more productive and prosperous venture.

Thus, when we look at the things we enjoy, things we do, things we pursue, and things we reflect upon, we come face to face with the question about what life holds for us. If life is such a pleasure to have, can its pleasure last? If the pleasure of life is lasting, can we have it forever and ever, even after we die? And, what is the pleasure of life about? Is it about the enjoyment of the material satisfaction of life, or is it about the satisfaction of the mind making sense of life? Or, is it something more and beyond, a yearning for a life everlasting, for instance, a life of yonder somewhere out there over the rainbow where pleasures overflow endlessly, forever and ever?

'And what is the life of this world except a fleeting of play and amusement, whereas the life of yonder in the hereafter is more glittering for those who are God-conscious. Do you then not reflect?' says the Qur'an in (6:32).

Life therefore is something that goes on but for us to live on and on and to be able to enjoy a life of bless and bliss continuously, we must first make our life on earth equally one of bless and bliss and to do that, we must seek to realize the very aim of our creation, namely, to be a human being of the most worthy kind who is wise, good, just, and beautiful and, never to forget that *Allah* is the point of reference for the realization of our human worthiness.

21

A Life of Both Worlds

*I*slam speaks of existence as *dunya* and *akhirah*. *Dunya* refers to what is near and *akhirah* to what is far. *Dunya* refers to this immediate world where we are living in right now. *Akhirah* refers to the world that we will find ourselves in after we die. *Dunya* is thus 'here' and *akhirah* is thus 'hereafter.'

One can say that there are three possible views on the relationship between *dunya* and *akhirah*. A first possible view is to regard that only *dunya* exists, not *akhirah*, because *dunya* is visible to us, a world that we can see, touch, feel, and enjoy. This, of course, is not the view of Islam.

A second possible view is to regard that both *dunya* and *akhirah* do indeed exist, with one leading up to the other, *dunya* leading up to *akhirah*. There is for us a world that we live right now with all its contents, and there is another world that awaits us, also with all its contents. We live a life of *dunya* to be followed by a life of *akhirah*.

A third possible view is to regard that both *dunya* and *akhirah* do indeed exist, with one leading up to the other, *dunya* leading up to *akhirah* but inasmuch as *akhirah* is a world of its own, *akhirah* is also the blueprint for the way *dunya* is. In this sense, the 'here' *is really* the 'hereafter.' *Dunya* and *akhirah* are two layers of existence glued to one another, but *dunya* will eventually wear and tear, and what remains is *akhirah*. Thus, one who lives a life of *dunya* is guided by the ideals of *akhirah* so that his life of *dunya* is modeled on the life of the *akhirah*. After he dies, he continues his life of *akhirah*, but this life will be determined by how much his life of *dunya* is carried out upon the ideals of *akhirah*.

Islam proposes a view of existence where underlying *dunya* is *akhirah*, the permanent but seemingly distant blueprint of *dunya*. It corresponds to the third view of the relationship between *dunya* and *akhirah* that is mentioned above.

Islam gives a very vivid and clear picture of what *akhirah* is like. *Akhirah* is the condition underlying *dunya*. The pleasant condition is called *jannah*. The unpleasant condition is called *naar*. *Jannah* is further described as that of a rosy place to be in, with its pleasant inhabitants and the delights of a beautiful life. This image of *jannah* serves as an imagery, a simile, an analogy, of how the world we live in should be organized. This world, the *dunya*, should be a carbon-copy of the *akhirah*. *Naar,* on the other hand, is given as a burning furnace, burning away all the blameworthy consequences that the self has accumulated when it was in *dunya*. The task of the self is to move from *dunya* to *akhirah* in the organization of its life, while the self is living life during the time it is in *dunya*.

◆

What goes around comes around, so goes a saying. If you do good, good will come to you. If you do bad, bad will come get you. If you do good, then good will come to you in *dunya*, but good will also come to you in *akhirah*. In the same way, if you do bad, bad will come to you in *dunya*, and bad will also come to you in *akhirah*. If you study hard for your exams, you will do well in your exams, and you will also get other good things in the distant time, such as getting a good job and a good salary for your good attitude towards studies. Likewise, if you do not study hard for your exams, do not expect to do well in your exams, and do not expect good things to come with your not-too-good attitude towards studies. 'You see all those guys that made it in this world,' your teacher would tell you, 'It is because they did good and did well in their studies.'

You see, your teacher uses a *future* example to make you understand your *present* condition. Your teacher tells you of how your seniors, those who have done well in their studies and careers, have gone on to lead a good life. You are still studying and do not know what your future holds for you. But at the same time, you get this sense of assurance that if you do good and do well in your studies, you will be like these people. You will one day arrive at where these people have arrived.

Islam is not opposed to all the enjoyment of things we have in this world. But Islam cautions that if our enjoyment of things is not governed by an underlying blueprint that gives us the idea of what these enjoyments mean, how these enjoyments should be pursued and enjoyed, and what these enjoyments will do to us in the future - we will end up finding ourselves saying one day, 'How I wish I had paid heed to all these things!' We find, for instance, many people smoking these days. Even the warning caption, along with the gory pictures of what happens from smoking, do not seem to deter these people from doing it. It is only when they suffer from health problems that they show remorse and regret. But they knew already about what is to come, and yet they chose to live this kind of present life.

◆

If we organize the world and our life according to the way it is, we get a sense of what *akhirah* is like. This world is an allusion to that world, so that when we lead a good life in this world, it gives us a sense of what better life awaits us in the hereafter. So if we have a sense of what little there is, we can look forward to what more there is that awaits us. If we have a home, and the home is one where the family members revere and respect each other, take care of each other, protect one another, and love each other, this is *jannah* on earth, this is *jannah* in *dunya*, and this will be our *jannah* in *akhirah*. If we have a home and the parents are often quarrelling with one another and the children are disrespectful to their parents, this is *naar* on earth, this is *naar* in *dunya*, and this will be *naar* in *akhirah*. If we know what it is like to have a blessed family, we know what *jannah* is going to be like. Likewise, if we know what a torturous family is like, we also know what *naar* is going to be like. *Jannah* has been pictured to us as such and such. *Naar* has been pictured to us as such and such. It's up to us to choose which one we want and apply it in our life here in this world.

For the self to be free in the true sense of the word, it is to be free from the sways and swerves of our human desires that give us the misperception that we are kings unto our own selves and that this world is our kingdom for us to enjoy indefinitely. Having freed ourselves from the cage of passions and from the misperception of what our existence constitutes, we move into the ultimate reality, into the embrace of God who is the real king and the real giver of existence, God who is the permanence of all that is. Only when we have moved from *dunya* to *akhirah* - making *akhirah* the blueprint of our life in this world - that we will be able to come to terms with the real nature of existence, with the real nature of who we are, with the real nature of our life in this world, and with the real nature of what awaits us after the impermanence of this world, this *dunya*, has left us. It is *akhirah* that awaits us, and behind *akhirah*, stands none other than God, who is the very source of *dunya* and *akhirah*, of us, of all that is.

22

A Life of Religion

Once upon a time, in many societies around the world, it would appear strange and awkward for someone living in those times to be told that religion is only one aspect and activity of the human life.

Rather, for that person, religion is everything. Religion *is* society, politics, economics, culture, education, art, and everything that has to do with human living, *all at once.* Religion or transcendent, cosmos or universe, Nature or environment, society and family, culture and ethics, self and body are inseparable from one another. Rather, they are all related as a web or chain of relationship, becoming mirror reflections of one another, and functioning as analogies for thought, feeling, and language. Even today, such as in the Malay language, one finds in the *peribahasa* or idiom, that someone is an *alim-alim kucing,* a 'pious-looking cat,' if he is a pretender.

Religion has existed from the very day our forefathers made their presence in this world. From the time the first humans emerged on earth, religion has always featured as a crucial dimension of human existence, giving us the story of our life - about where we came from, what we are doing in this world, and where we will be going after we die. It is only in modern times like ours that the view of religion as the need of the oppressed, the assurance of the weak-minded, and the salvation of the hapless came about. Religion is equated with myth, superstition and things primitive. It is a thing of the past and can never feature in modern life that hails reason and science as liberation from religion. Religion is seen as old things, old ways, old habits, and all things outdated and obsolete, and these things, at best, serve only as precious mementos for museum display.

However, when we turn to a modern scholar of religion such as Emile Durkheim, whom every student of sociology is acquainted with, we will be astounded to find that the way Durkheim describes religion is as applicable to modern societies as it is to past or even primitive societies. For Durkheim, the essence of religion is the 'sacred,' a quality that holds everything together in a unity so that if this quality is lost, then everything will collapse and become separate entities that do not have a common identity. For primitive people, the sacred appears as the 'totem,' a name for the sacred as the unifying principle and function of whatever there is in existence. Because the totem cannot be seen or touched, an emblem, which is a visual image, is used to represent the totem. This emblem usually takes the form of an animal. If the emblem is a lion, then the sacred is visualized as a terrifying and brave power. This emblem becomes the emblem of a group or clan, so that all the members in that group or clan visualize the sacred as a lion. Following this, the members of the group or clan also visualize themselves as a lion, and their behaviour and movement imitate that of the lion.

Although modern people no longer think of religion this way, yet, in many ways, their behaviour reflects this characteristic of religion. Take, for example, a football club. The club's emblem brings together its fans into a unity of the club's image so that if the emblem is tarnished in any way, the fans would react to the incident, sometimes even to the point of going into a fight. This shows that the emblem is actually a totem and holds a special place in the minds and hearts of the fans, so special that it acquires a 'sacred' status to the extent that doing anything harmful to the emblem means also incurring the wrath of the club and its fans.

◆

The past and the present may appear to us as different instances of existence, one considered less and the other more in civilizational achievements, but if looked at in the proper light, there are many things in common between the past and the present that made religion as vibrant and relevant even for those who think the modern has left religion behind in the name of progress and enlightenment.

Religion, if it has been thought of as a thing of the past, can be thought of as a thing of the present, if only we understand how the connection is made. Take the mosque and the Western-style eateries, for instance.

Today, Western fast-food outlets have become synonymous with Muslim lifestyle. Muslims, young and old alike, like to frequent places like Pizza Hut, Burger King, A&W, Starbucks, and other such places, and eating pizzas, hot dogs, and burgers have become a local habit these days. But these places carry with them Western names and, historically and culturally, Western things are foreign to the Muslim experience of religion. So what have Pizza Hut and Burger King got to do with religion?

Restaurants and eateries with Western names nonetheless can be places where religion happens. Western-style eating outlets can be regarded as 'a place of worship' the same way the mosque is a place of worship because a place of worship is a place where goodness happens, and eating food that is healthy to the body is an act of goodness.

While names are important because they reflect what identity a restaurant carries, as long as the name is not one that touches on the sensitivities of the Muslim faith, they should not be a problem. Muslims in Malaysia and Singapore, for instance, are sensitive to dogs, but they have no problem eating hot dog. But if the restaurant is called 'Doggy Restaurant' then the restaurant should not expect Muslim customers.

Apart from names, as long as the food is *halal*, or permissible from the viewpoint of the Islamic dietary laws, the restaurant can be considered a religious place for Muslims. There is a misunderstanding however regarding what *halal* is. *Halal* is not pork-free or lard-free or no pork served. Whether it is beef or chicken, *halal* beef or chicken refers to meat prepared according to the Islamic dietary laws and if they are not, they cannot be consumed.

For a restaurant to be a religious place, it is not enough for the food to be *halal*. The food must also be nutritious and of good quality, the place has to be hygienic and comfortable, and the services have to be prompt and appealing. It is these 'extras' that made many people, both young and old as well as the little ones, to want to come to Western-style restaurants to eat because they have the recipe to attract people to their places. They have quality control.

Muslim scholars right from the days when Islam blossomed to become a world civilization have classified Islamic daily living into three broad categories. These are *daruriyyat* or necessary, *hajiyyat* or desirable, and *tahsiniyyat* or premium lifestyle. To be able to savour a piece of chicken so that one could go on living is *daruriyyat*. But nobody wants to eat just to avoid being hungry. They want to see the chicken properly cooked, tastes juicy, the meat is tender, and, of course, nice to see and whets the appetite. This is *hajiyyat*. But above all, the appetite becomes a full picture of a culture when one sees what culinary art could do to make the chicken dish something that trains a person to be a cultured personality with the way he sits around the table, how he behaves towards the food before, during, and after meals, and how he keeps his manners when he is eating. This is *tahsiniyyat*.

Therefore, meals and restaurants could be religious things because they serve out the purpose of religious living which is to make a person conscientious about his manners and ethics of everyday living which would then mould him into a personality desired by religion.

◆

For Muslims, religion is everyday, everywhere, and everything, past and present, traditional and modern. Religion occurs even to a restaurant through which we live our religious existence, fulfill our social meaning, and portray our human identity.

When we put all these things of everyday living together, from mosque to restaurant to school to hospital and even to attire and to pen, we will see that they are linked in such a way as to form a religious matrix connecting these things as religious. Only then, religion appears to us as a total and complete way of life. Mankind has always been religious from day one of their existence. It is they who need to know that they have been religious all along, even in modern times like ours.

23

A Life of Islam

What is one doing when he or she chooses a life of Islam? To choose a life of Islam is to choose to become a human being of the noblest and finest kind, one who is called *khalifah*.

In today's world, whenever the word *khalifah* is mentioned, it immediately brings to mind the idea of an Islamic state with a leader who brandishes his sword and waves his flag of conquer and intimidation. It is, so to speak, a word that sends chills down the spine and the fear that comes out of it.

On the contrary, a *khalifah* is a vicegerent of God on earth, one who assumes his existence on earth as a trust (called *amanah*) from heaven to make the world a delightful place to live, for himself as well as for others.

To make the world a delightful place to live, we must first of all, every single one of us, be a delightful personality in the first place! And what is a delightful personality? A delightful personality is a personality of *jannah*, a personality that makes the earthly life brims with the heavenly sunshine, a life where we live in co-existence with others whether humans or otherwise and not one where we shed blood and cause destruction to lives, properties, and the greeneries. For that, we must, first and foremost, recognize our status as *khalifah*, that we are the servants of *Allah* carrying out the trust to prosper earth with goodness and love and not litter it with enmity and hatred.

To realize our status as *khalifah* and to acquire a personality of *jannah*, we turn our direction to *Allah*. After all, it is *Allah* who brought us into existence and He is the source of our sustenance as well as the centre of guidance through which we blossom into our human meaning, carry that meaning into our everyday living, and from which we able to grow into a wholesome human being.

As such, we need to be in touch with *Allah* so that His guiding light can penetrate into our soul and spirit, enlighten our mind and body, illuminate our psychology and personality, and navigate our action and interaction.

Allah guides us through the Qur'an and the Sunnah, the Qur'an being the very word of God and the Sunnah being Prophet Muhammad's utterances and speeches, acts, and activities that purport to show how the Qur'an is lived in everyday living.

With the Qur'an and the Sunnah, the Muslim has a guiding light but to follow the light, it is not enough to merely follow what it says and what it shows. Rather, we have to participate in the light and help determine whether it is going to shine bright or becoming a dim light.

We humans are endowed with the intellect called 'aql and with this precious gift from heaven, we can now participate in making this world a wonderful place to live in.

The role of the intellect is to find a meeting point between the Qur'an and the Sunnah on the one hand, and what we observe with our eyes of the things that surround our living.

The things around us serve as ayat or signs that point to their farther and further meanings and by following the trails of their meanings, we can come to a meeting point between these meanings with the intents of the Qur'an and the Sunnah and therefore obtain a clear picture of the message of Islam to our living.

With a clear picture about how we go about with living through the Qur'an and the Sunnah that is worked out and laid out with the mind, we can then apply the intents of the heavenly wisdom into our day to day action and interaction.

Our day to day actions and interactions pertain to the fulfillment of our varieties of need without which we cannot function as a human being as well as able to continue living, and these needs range from the biological to the intellectual to the aesthetical and to the spiritual.

Our acts and activities however are done not merely for us to be able to eat, sleep, and shelter. Water is necessary to the survival of life but we humans are not contented with only having water to drink. We drink water but water that also appears as coffee, tea, and all kinds of drinks. Needless to say, we are a species unlike the birds and beasts where we are able to turn the raw material of the environment into items for life's fulfillment that come in all kinds of varieties and names as well as for all kinds of purposes. Life will be tasteless if it is monotonous and lacks meaningfulness and therefore, culture is needed if life is to be colourful and thus delightful to savour. With culture, we drink water that comes as all kinds of beverages and drink them to fulfill religious, social, or recreational meanings and purposes.

A life of Islam is a life of worship or *ibadah*. A Muslim is one who is always in worship of *Allah*, irrespective of what, where, and when. All his activities as well as cultural practices, are acts of worship. Nothing that a Muslim does is not worship. Prayer is worship but so is watching news on TV. The mosque is a place of worship but so is a restaurant where religion also happens.

In other words, worship carries a rather broad meaning and apart from the specific acts carried out with a total focus on God alone, acts pertaining to relationships with other things and other creatures of God are also considered as worship. Eating, learning, working, and playing too are acts of worship because these have to be carried out to bring about praiseworthy consequences to life and living.

Put it more specifically, specific acts of worship such as the prayer and general acts of worship such as drinking or gardening are connected with one another as a total and complete sense of worship through (1) the intention which is to do it in God's name as it is God who is the giver and sustainer of life, (2) the goodness of the act which is to bring benefit to the one doing the act or activity, and (3) the sincerity with regard to the purpose of the act or activity which is to benefit others and not for any ulterior motives such as to promote one's self-centredness.

Irrespective of what an act or activity or cultural practice is, it must be guided by the Qur'an and the Sunnah through the principles of *tawhid* and *shariah*.

Tawhid and *shariah* supply the virtues of living so that in whatever we aspire and desire, we are always kept in touch about not losing our human value and letting our humanity slips away.

When we are conscious that God is ever present in our life, we will be careful and try not to be arrogant and selfish to our fellow humans and also not behave towards them in unbecoming manners. Rather, by understanding God's significance in our life, we will instead practise caring and sharing, as well as loving and sacrificing. That is precisely the wisdom of God in our life, that we do not only see ourselves as a dominant and dominating creature over all others that exist alongside us, but rather, see our presence as a co-existence with others. We are, so to speak, a creature of togetherness.

Togetherness however is not only with our fellow humans. We are bonded also with the skies and seas, rivers and streams, meadows and greeneries, as well as the birds and beasts. These creatures of Nature are our life's sustenance but they also serve as pointers, as *ayat*, about life's purpose.

And what is life's purpose? Is it about the enjoyment of life? If it is, what is the enjoyment of life about? Eat, drink and be merry before the angel of death snatches our soul and returns it to the heavenly abode? Is it lamenting about the trials and tribulations we humans have to face in trying to build a life on earth? Is it about getting away from family and friends and go to a faraway place to lead a solitary life of peace and quietude?

We humans are endowed with the intellect to reflect upon the purpose of life. With the intellect, we can think for ourselves what life is all about. With the intellect, we can also inquire about the reasons behind God creating the world.

A life of Islam is a life where God is a blessing rather than a hindrance in our existence. The more we are into God, the more we become reflective and curious about our life's purpose and therefore, we become more intelligent and also more praiseworthy in our conduct and behaviour because we know what it is and what it means to exist as a human being.

As such, a life of Islam is a life where we build a life of paradise on earth before we move on to the paradise in heaven after our demise and to build such a life where heaven is constructed on earth, we need to live, interact, and work alongside all that is part of our existence, from our fellow humans to our partners in the ecology or environment and to God, for without them, we would not be able to bring the joy of living into light and as a consequence, we will not be able to become a *khalifah* who will delight the world with his personality of *jannah*, a personality of heaven made on earth.

Moreover, each and every one of us is a personality with four selves that together constitute our personal identity, and these are me (my very own self), we (with other fellow humans), us (with the world of Nature), and all (with God and the spiritual beings). Therefore, I am who I am because of who we all are. Or, as the Three Musketeers would say, 'All for one, and one for all'.

And that is what a life of Islam is about, that in existing, we move from living to meaning to being human in the noblest of meaning, and to move from here to there, we look to *Allah* as the centre through which His guiding light shines through our intellect and intelligence and makes us see things in clear perspective about how we go about with life, how we relate to others, and how we become a human being who is worthy to be called *khalifah*, God's vicegerent on earth.

And unless we make ourselves worthy to live a life of heaven on earth, we cannot expect a vacancy for heaven to admit us into its garden after our time on earth has expired.

24

A Chinese Life of Islam

*F*or a Malaysian Muslim of Chinese descent like myself, an understanding of *tawhid* will not be adequate if it is not seen also in the context of the Chinese experience of religion.

The Chinese view of existence, religion, and life is structured around the notion of *Tian Ren He Yi* or Harmony of Heaven and Human.

Chinese indigenous religion, the religion of most of the Chinese around the world, has no idea of God like the one in Islam. The closest one can find to the idea of God in Islam in the Chinese religious worldview is *Tian* or Heaven. Other than this, the Chinese believe in *shen*, spirits and deities, who took on human form and appear as magistrates, warriors, scholars, and benevolent persons, such as Kuan Yin, the female goddess of mercy, and they live on the 'clouds on high' very up in the sky. One can find altars inside or outside the homes, offices, shops, or construction sites that house images of these *shen* for the purpose of procuring blessings, protection, and safety to the residential or business premises. Joss-sticks, Chinese tea in small cups, and fruits are usually placed at the altars.

Religion, for the Chinese, is not about a creator of the multitude of things such that all things in existence, humans in particular, have to acknowledge this creator, as well as worshipping it according to certain patterns of conduct, otherwise the faith or belief of a person can be rendered null and void. Although, for the Chinese, religion is about the presence of the supernatural in their lives, it is the *functional* aspect of the presence that matters to them instead of whether the supernatural has to be such-and-such a deity with such-and-such a feature. Irrespective of who or what a 'god' is, that 'god' must be a practical god, one that answers the needs of mankind, brings good tidings and things to them, and keeps harm and calamity away from their lives. Human beings, on their part, must behave in ways that will ensure the balance and harmony of the world they inhabit, as there are personal and social norms to be followed, such as children having to be filial to their parents, or those living having to 'serve' their dead ancestors through not shaming them with their conduct.

Religion, for the Chinese, is a harmonious co-existence between heaven and human i.e. between *Tian* and human, and it is for 'earth' (in modern times like ours, this is taken to be the law of Nature) to mediate between them, providing the way where heaven and human can relate to one another for the continuity of existence and for peace to prevail over skies, lands, and seas, and where human beings order their lives and surroundings according to the law of Nature based on the *yin* and *yang* forces. Thus, religion is the mutual co-existence, inter-dependence, and balance between heaven, earth, and human, between the living and the dead, and between deities and seekers of blessings and peace.

◆

As it is said, *Tian* comes closest to the notion of God in Islam. *Tian* appears as heaven and sky. As heaven, it is the focus for the procurement of blessing and bliss, peace and prosperity, calmness of mind and serenity of heart. As sky, it pours down rain for plants to grow and gifts water for humans and cattle to drink. But *Tian* also instructs human beings about ways of living and behaving. This is called *Tian Ming*, Mandate or Decree of Heaven. This is done through a human appointment, and it is usually the King, who receives the mandate and discharges it upon his subjects or citizens. As such, the king is called *Tian Zi* or 'Son of Heaven.' The common folks i.e. subjects and citizens, who follow these instructions, are called *Tian Xia*, All Under Heaven.

Confucius (Kong Zi), who lived in the 6th century BCE and whose name became synonymous with Chinese culture and civilization known as Confucianism, looked to the rulers of the Zhou dynasty as the ideal figures of the Chinese way in religion, culture, and values, and whether this is a correct interpretation or not, Confucianism came to embody the Chinese spirit, mind, and attitude.

Chinese rulers, in very ancient times, do not rule by whims and fancies, but are governed by a set of behaviour set by Heaven. If they fail to follow Heaven's wishes and mandate, and are bent on committing injustices towards their subjects, undesirable consequences could befall upon the rulers. As such, the kings were guided by a group of advisers who knew how to communicate with *Tian*, and they also knew the decorum of the palace conduct, instructing the kings about correct behaviour towards heaven and humans. These were the *Ru*, experts on the rituals of life.

Confucius was said to have learnt from the *Ru* and he prized highly their art and science of living that gives emphasis on the meaning of being human as the gift from heaven. To be human is the essence of the Confucian teaching and this would later become the central philosophy and worldview of the Chinese.

Throughout the whole teaching of Confucianism, *ren* (written as 仁) or being-human*ness* is the aim of human living and this can only be realized through constant learning and practising the way of heaven as the way of human.

Thus, the Chinese understanding of being human that is grounded on the Confucian vision of humanity is one where being human is not detached from heaven's way but rather heaven's way is put into practice through the person manifesting the virtues, called *de* or *te*, that were already innate and present in the human self but only waiting to be brought out into the open. It is when one acts according to the proper manner of behaving, can these virtues be manifested and seen. Otherwise, these virtues may appear dim and opaque and may eventually lose their strength and vitality to manifest strongly in the character of a person.

In order for the virtues to manifest in a person, the family is considered the most important locus for developing one's personality. Besides the family, community's involvement and self-cultivation on the part of the individual are also required to make the effort fruitful and realizable. Needless to say, religion, in the Chinese context, is about bringing out the good-natured self of an individual to become a wholesome character and a praiseworthy personality that he will end up as a good person, a filial child, a useful citizen, and a worthy endowment of heaven.

◆

When a Malaysian of Chinese descent steps into Islam, he sees *Tian* as more than just a source of his sustenance. That *Tian* has everything to do with his life means, for him, that *Tian* is also the source of his existence.

Tian cannot only be implored and sought for this and that and that is all to Its worth. Ask a father or mother who showers their children with love and care, and having to put up with their antics and erratics, whether it is acceptable for them that the children choose to ignore or even refuse to listen to their advice.

Parents will go the distance to sacrifice whatever it takes to make sure their children get to eat well, sleep well, and be well in everything, but their sacrifices will mean nothing to them if they do not feel their children's recognition of them as parents. Even to the extent where the children become negligent of their parents' welfare and well-being, still, for the parents, nothing matters more than this—recognize me as your parent, and know that I am your father or mother.

If such is the nature between parents and children, what more when it comes to humans and the One they plead for the good things in life. Doesn't *Tian* deserve more than just being a sanctuary to seek blessings and good things of life?

For a Malaysian Muslim of Chinese descent, *Tian* is not only the focus for procuring benefits. Rather, *Tian* is recognized first, with regard to who He is, and thereafter, with regard to His power and dominion through which existence becomes possible, life becomes realizable, and good things become thinkable. Only then can it be said that *Tian,* now recognized as *Allah,* covers the full meaning of the One as both *God,* namely, He is what He is and *Lord,* He is the giver and caretaker of everything.

◆

In the Chinese understanding of religion, religion is the workings of *Tian* in human life, whether at the personal, family, or community level.

For instance, *Tian* expresses its presence in the family through *xiao* or filial piety. *Xiao* is respect and reverence for parents. It is a virtue that in practising it, one is realizing the *Tian Ming*, Mandate of Heaven where *Tian* imparts this virtue in the hearts of human beings to be brought out into their character and personality and therefore fulfilling *Tian's* desire for the realization of the true human being.

Thus, to exhibit *xiao* is to execute the instruction of *Tian Ming*, and it is basically to realize *Tian* in life's workings so that *Tian* can be seen present in our daily living.

Needless to say, in the Chinese context, religion is visible

when one sees the operation and fulfillment of the brilliant
virtues—in family, person, and community—because these
virtues are the connecting points between human and heaven
that in bringing them out from the depth of one's psychology
into the surface of one's behaviour and character, one opens
the gate of one's self for *Tian* to pass through into the heart,
mind, body, and spirit, so that there will be a synchronicity
between heaven's mandate and human will, and actions will
have positive consequences, and *Tian Ren He Yi*, Harmony of
Heaven and Human, will have been realized, and religion
would have served its meaning and purpose. This concept of
religion is not easy to grasp and therefore it is not surprising
that for some people, the Chinese only have ethics but not
religion.

◆

Religion, in the Chinese context, is not something that could
be seen right before one's eyes. However it can be grasped
through looking at the workings of religion in human life.

In and within concrete and particular situations, the
Chinese sense the presence of religion. Arguments to prove the
existence of God or why God is one will not so much move
their hearts in the direction towards the All-Mighty, but
practical workings of religion in life's situations and the
positive consequences coming out from them will enable them
to grasp and sense religion's relevance to their existence. To
illustrate the point, mention GOD and one gets the idea of a
supreme being that looms over the life of humans. For a
Chinese, he looks at GOD separately as G, O, and D and sees

the relevance of each letter to his life through which he makes out God's presence and senses His meaningfulness and practical consequences to him. For one who sees God only when God strikes him as GOD, he cannot sense the presence of God if God strikes him as G, O, D separately because G, O, and D are dispersed and do not seem to present as a single concept. To a Chinese however, he sees G, O, D as mirrors to one another through which he connects their separate positions by looking at how one letter reflects the contents of the others and how, together, they form a unity of meaning that presents to him the unity of God's presence.

◆

For a Malaysian Muslim of Chinese descent (Malaysian Chinese Muslims are predominantly converts to Islam), *Tian Ren He Yi* can be a useful medium to enhance his understanding and practice of Islam. For that, he needs to understand how *tawhid* stands as the core virtue through which *Tian Ren He Yi* is realizable.

The first thing he needs to know about *tawhid* is that whatever he pursues in this worldly life, the rewards that he reaps will continue even after he dies. Thus the hard work he puts into making his life in this world a fulfilling venture is not going to end after he dies. Rather, the efforts he puts into the work are going to count towards his well-being in his next life. Therefore, the life on earth should be made joyous, enjoyable, and vibrant as much as possible, and, how pleasurable and pleasant is the worldly life here, it will be much more in the hereafter.

Therefore, he should work hard, be industrious, productive, and forward looking about his prospects in life, and he should also enjoy the fruits of his labour, savouring the sweetness of his pursuits of life.

But he should know that excessiveness of things can be derogatory to his well-being. Needless to say, his humanity or *ren* could suffer and he could regress into becoming a kind of person who may be lacking in his self-worth and dignity, a kind of person others would rather not associate with. One development arising out of excessiveness is greediness, which in turn would lead to selfishness, which in turn would lead to self-centredness, and which in turn would lead to self-pride or egoism called *kibr*, making one to see himself as the centre of everything and others as less valuable in comparison to him. When a person has a big ego, he thinks only of himself, thinks that whatever he says is all that matters, and thinks that his actions are the only correct ones. He disregards others and brushes away their importance, and easily gets agitated or angry if he is told of his weaknesses. When one has developed egoism to a high degree, not only humans will he disregard, even laws he will not obey, and beyond that, even God he will behave petty towards.

As such, one must not allow his self to develop into an ego destructive to his personality that will also be detrimental to the well-being of others. He must make his humanity to become a praiseworthy personality, and this he can achieve by bringing out the virtues in his heart and nurturing them, strengthening them, and brightening them until they become illuminating lights in his body, mind, character, personality, behaviour, action, interaction, and communication.

Ren, humanity or being human, is the objective of the Chinese life. To be a person of *ren*, for a Malaysian Chinese Muslim, is to bring *tawhid* into fruition in all aspects of his existence and way of living, as *tawhid* provides the impetus, guidelines, and direction for the realization and functioning of his humanity and human meaning. With *Allah* standing as the reference point for his human becoming, he is able to see himself more clearly and aptly who he is as a human being.

Thus, *tawhid* is a very significant virtue through which we understand our place in existence, our relationship with all that exists and their contributions to our efforts, successes, and well-being, and finally, our human meaning and becoming through which *Allah* stands at the centre of our humanity without which we can drift into egoism and as a result, bring destruction to ourselves and others but more significantly, bring destruction to *ren* and all the other virtues in our personality that characterize our living, meaning, and being human.

As such, for a Chinese, to be a Muslim is not to abandon his Chinese roots and legacy, but it is to align those noble elements of the Chinese heritage with the Islamic principles of *tawhid* and *shariah*, as well as *akhirah*.

Tian Ren He Yi can be the philosophical foundation of the outlook of life and the guidelines for living for a Chinese who makes Islam his path of life as, after all, its teachings, traits, qualities, and elements are what we find inborn in our *fitrah*, those good-natured seeds of humanity present in us the moment we were born into this world.

25

A Life Worth Asking About

*I*f *Allah* is the answer to why we exist, why did He bring us into the world, give us life, and then take it from us? Why did *Allah* create a world that spreads before our eyes with all its temptations and then give us a little time with it and after sometime it is time to say goodbye? Why then give life? What is life for? What is life about?

Life is *Allah's* pride because He created it but it is also something we find it worth having and wouldn't want to forego it because we know that it is a precious and valuable thing the moment we have it. But the worthiness of life and the satisfaction of having it will only be realized once we know how, with God, we can become that something called human being.

Thus, to have God is not to be in bondage like a slave and a master but to be in a relationship with *Allah* who stands as that pivotal point through which His wisdom and knowledge, love and compassion, goodness and mercifulness, and beauty and perfection are reflected into our life so that we can become a human being who is wise, good, loving, and beautiful, those heavenly virtues and values that all of us undeniably desire having.

Allah wants us to be wonderful and beautiful, physically and spiritually, inwardly and outwardly, character-wise and behaviour-wise. Beauty is the culmination and epitome of all that is complete, good, and perfect. In this sense, to be a beautiful human being is the very essence of our existence, humanity and human personality for God Himself will be proud that His most loved of creations reflects what He loves most for Himself. We come into this world as a beautiful creation in the form of a baby who is cute and charming but an empty vessel that needs filling and we shall return to that world of our origin filled with a beautiful personality. That is what life is for and about, namely, to become a beautiful human being. If we can understand why we humans love beauty then we can understand why beauty is everything to *Allah*.

Allah gave us this life in order for us to have a taste of what a better life promises, but that will have to wait until we die. For now, we need to appreciate this life that our breath is holding, and be grateful for the enjoyment that it is giving, but an enjoyment that will make us into a beautiful creature worthy to live in that place that goes on and on without stopping, a place called *jannah* or paradise.

In order for us to have a wonderful life, we are gifted with the mind. We could tell ourselves and say, 'Wouldn't it be wonderful that life is one by which we are given everything for living without having to think and work for it but that we close our eyes and pray and when we open our eyes, everything is laid right before us falling from the sky! This is indeed paradise!'

But that is not how things work. *Allah* wants us to use the mind because He wants us to know that a wonderful life is one by which we are involved in the process of its creation and that our participation in constructing and designing the life we dream of having is for us to appreciate the worthiness of our own creation and not merely that we rely solely on heaven to set out every minute detail about how things should work out for living.

Needless to say, God wants us to know that a wonderful life is heaven, earth, and human working together in unison to carve out a paradise on earth that would be pleasing to God and make us humans feeling worthy of our existence.

But that wonderful life can only be wonderful if and only if we make God the centre of our existence and allow the sunshine of divine guidance pierces into our mind and body that will then animate our thought and feeling into awakening everything around us to construct a paradise for living but a paradise that is filled with the kind of human being we all yearn to be, namely, one who knows that the centrality of God in his life is blessing and bliss to his existence and not a burden and pain to his human becoming, that God is a joy to be with and not a sorrow to lament from.

Index

Angels (*mala'ikah*) 21
  views of humans, 21, 22
  difference with humans,
  23, 25

Allah
  notion, 7-8
  connection to human, 7
  centre of life, 12, 13, 102
  relevance, 103

amal salih, 15, 19
  relation to work, 86
  guidelines, 86
  maslaha, 86
  purpose, 90

Ayat (signs), 68
  relation to God, 68-69

Centre
  significance, 11-12

Culture
  meaning, 53-55
  adab, ta'dib, 55-56

Existence, 110
  as *dunya* and *akhirah*, 110
  relationship between
  them, 110-112
  relationship to *jannah* and
  naar, 113

fardhu ain, 48
    essential elements, 48-51

Halal, 18
    misunderstanding, 118

Ibadah, 15
    intention (*niyyah*), 27
    worship, 17, 26
    wider meaning, 17,18, 26,
    124
    prerequisites, 27
    relation with *khalifah*, 17,
    19
    relation with *adat*, 80-81

Intellect (*'aql*), 88
    third element, 92
    relation to Qur'an and
    Sunnah, 93-99
    relationship with mind,
    104

Isti'mar, 15
    prospering, 19

jannah (paradise, heaven)
    connection to earth, 108

Khalifah, 15
    vicegerent, 16, 121
    comparison with angels,
    23
    Adam, 22
    intelligence, 23-24
    forgetfulness, 24
    unity of existence, 16
    person of culture, 56

Learning
    purpose of learning, 76-79
    two sets of knowledge, 79-
    80

Masjid (mosque)
    centrality in human life, 12

muhlikat, 81

munjiyat, 81

najasah (impurity), 39

Nature
    variety of meanings, 62-65
    as signs, 66, 68

Prayer (*solat*)
  prophetic sayings, 30, 35
  function, 30, 31, 32
  connection to life, 34

Prophets, 41
  mission, 41

Purity
  five forms, 37

Self
  nafs, 87
  relationship with God, 8-10
  four selves, 57

Sincerity (*ikhlas*)
  meaning, 44
  elements that destroy, 45-48

Shariah, 86
  maqasid al-shariah, 86

Sunnah, 92

taqwa, 59
  basis of togetherness, 59

Tawhid, see *Allah*
  purification, 39

Tian, notion 130, 133
  purpose, 132

Tian Ren He Yi, 135
  relation with *tawhid*, 135, 137

Togetherness
  reason for, 58-59
  unity of, 60-61

Work
  variety of meanings, 82-83
  fulfillment of needs, 84-85
  amal salih, 86
  purpose, 90